Kim Frazer

Gaining the Mental Edge at Bridge

Honors Books is an imprint of Master Point Press. All contents, editing and
design (excluding cover design) are the sole responsibility of the authors.

Master Point Press
214 Merton St. Suite 205
Toronto, Ontario, Canada
M4S 1A6
(647) 956-4933

info@masterpointpress.com

www.masterpointpress.com
www.bridgeblogging.com
www.teachbridge.com
www.ebooksbridge.com

ISBN: 978-1-77140-210-1

Cover Design: Olena S. Sullivan/New Mediatrix

1 2 3 4 5 6   22 21 20 19

For John who is my greatest supporter

Contents

Foreword

This bridge book is unlike any other that you have read. You will not find a new bidding system or conventions or lessons on play as declarer or tips on opening leads or defence. There are already plenty of books on those subjects.

Instead, you will find plenty of invaluable advice on how to maximise your potential by what you do before play even starts, how to bring out your best during the session, how to recognise and eliminate negative thinking, how to deal with conflict at the bridge table, how to relax after a bridge session is over and be at your peak the next day, and much more. You will have come across many of the situations reported and which can arise during a bridge session. You might even recognise yourself.

Kim Frazer, a gold medallist in shooting competitions at international level, brings her wealth of knowledge and experience to show you how to apply similar principles and behaviour at the bridge table. Here is a winner giving you advice on what you can do to win, too. In the same way that she used these mental skills to succeed in her shooting, so Kim illustrates how you can use and benefit from the same skills at bridge.

Just as every individual is different, you might find that not every suggestion is suitable for you. Still, there are so many ideas that can lift your game and improve your results, it would be sensible to try to apply as much of Kim's advice as you can. Since bridge is a mental game, whatever you can do to stimulate and boost your mental prowess must be worth adopting.

Some of the concepts in this book are already part of my training routine, but there are also some that I have not seen before. I am anxious to try out these new ideas and incorporate them as part of my regular regime.

I can't wait for my next bridge game! I would just like to bar all of my regular opponents from reading this book.

Ron Klinger

2019

Introduction

Since the early 1970's there has been an explosion of understanding in the area of sports psychology with sports psychologists now readily accessible to help athletes with the mental side of their game. There is also a large amount of material on sports psychology available online and in libraries and bookshops. I am neither a sports psychologist, nor a psychologist of any kind. However, I have acquired a lot of knowledge that helped me to win at international target shooting, and which I believe can also be applied at the bridge table and more broadly.

My initial involvement with sports psychology started in the mid-1980s when I was invited to join the National Development Squad for Target Rifle Shooting. The squad participated in a one-week training camp held at the Australian Institute of Sport (AIS) in Canberra, Australia, and it was here that I was first introduced to the mental side of sport. At that time, the AIS was using sports psychologists to help teams. One of these sports psychologists (Graham Winter) had worked extensively with some of the Australian shooting team that competed at the 1980 Olympic Games in Moscow. One of the shooters who had taken his ideas on board was a coach at the camp, and she spoke about mental training. It was the first time I heard of the concepts of visualisation and imagery being systematically applied to help improve shooting skills.

A couple of years later, an American friend whom I had met while competing overseas sent me a series of audio tapes which had been recorded when the top American shooter and Olympic gold medallist, Lanny Bassham, had travelled to Canberra and worked with some of the National Squad. His series of tapes were enormously influential on my development as an international shooter. Over the next 20 years, I read more on the topic from a variety of sources. Lanny has gone on to make a business out of delivering seminars on Mental Management Systems[1]. I acknowledge the significant part his work has played in both my success as a shooter and in my understanding of the mental side of sport.

After retiring from competitive shooting, I took up bridge, which I had played a few times while at university. Second time around, I fell in love with the game which has become a passion for me. A chance conversation with the captain of the Australian Open team in 2013 led me to consider how mental management techniques could be used in bridge. This in turn has led to a series of articles on mental management in the Australian Bridge Federation's bi-monthly newsletter and in the Australian Bridge magazine. However, newsletters and magazines don't lend themselves to in-depth discussion, and so the articles have been expanded and turned into this book.

In writing this book I have drawn upon the knowledge I have acquired during my sporting career and translated it into practical uses at the card table, particularly in my chosen game of bridge. More generally, the concepts can be applied to any card or board game, as well as other aspects of sport and life.

Since my background is sport—specifically target rifle shooting— I have used several examples from different sports which may be familiar to many and assist with illustrating the points being made.

Naturally, since this is a book about mental tools for bridge, it would hardly be complete without a few bridge hands to illustrate particular points, but you won't find loads of analysis on how to play, defend or bid each particular hand. There are hundreds of books on these topics and much better players than me to write them. The situations depicted in the hands in this book are all real and nearly all are hands I and/or one of my partners have played or defended, but I have left the other players anonymous for obvious reasons.

---

1   mentalmanagement.com

I have also included some very basic technical material on sports psychology and psychology in general. This information is generally detailed in boxes. It's not necessary to know the underlying theory in order for you to use mental management, but this material is there for the people who are interested, along with some references for further reading if you want to find out more on any particular topic.

Finally, I thought it might be useful to include some tips on training, goal setting, training plans and other aspects that were common methods I used in my sport. If you want to take your competition to the next level and put in more effort, you might find these chapters helpful in guiding your bridge training.

Although this book has been written with bridge players in mind, the tools and concepts are applicable to any mind-game activity—whether it is poker, chess, backgammon or any of the other competitively played card and board games. Not everything in this book is for everyone, and what one player needs, another may have little use for—but I would be surprised if you didn't find something useful in these pages. Just like you decide which bridge method you use, you must evaluate what is best for you to help you to deal with your own weaknesses and enable you to play at your best!

Chapter 1

Why is Mental Management Important?

"I always felt that my greatest asset was not my physical ability — it was my mental ability."

- Bruce Jenner, Olympic gold medallist (decathlon)

Dealer: East
Vulnerable: EW

```
                        ♠ 64
                        ♥ AK5
                        ♦ Q109752
                        ♣ K5
        ♠ J75                       ♠ K10832
        ♥ 86                        ♥ Q32
        ♦ 643                       ♦ J8
        ♣ AQJ92                     ♣ 643
                        ♠ AQ9
                        ♥ J10974
                        ♦ AK
                        ♣ 1087
```

West	North	East	South
		Pass	1NT
Pass	3NT	All pass	

North-South were playing a 15-17 no-trump and South became declarer in three no-trumps.

West led the queen of clubs. With this club-suit combination, playing the king is the correct play. It gains whenever the ace is onside or if East has the nine of clubs. Yet on this hand our expert declarer failed at trick one by ducking and the defence took the first five tricks to defeat what should have been a cold contract.

This is a hand where clear thinking would have led the player in question to the right decision, yet an expert player failed when faced with the problem at the table. We use phrases like 'he had a brain fade' or 'she had a blind spot' to describe this kind of situation. If you are reading this book, you are interested in reducing these sorts of things happening to yourself and your partner.

Let's have a look at why mental skills are important to competitive bridge players.

Bridge is a game with many facets. To be successful, a player needs to achieve a high degree of skill in each of these facets—whether it is technical ability, partnership understanding or agreements, concentration, match fitness and stamina in a long tournament and other factors which go into being a good bridge player. I believe having strong mental skills is simply one of these facets.

It is now widely recognised in sport that strong technical skills alone are not enough to win. While the players who are successful must possess strong technical skills, they must also pay attention to other areas such as mental training and preparation and allied areas like nutrition, recovery and so on.

Strong mental skills allow sportspeople to perform at their best. The concept of improving mental skills to enhance performance has now been translated into many fields and used by many different professions such as business people, surgeons, fighter pilots, public speakers and so on.

In his book 'Outliers[1]', Malcolm Gladwell set the benchmark of 10,000 hours as the magic amount of training or effort required to achieve a high

---

1   Outliers, M. Gladwell: 2008 Χηαπτερ 2.

level of expertise in a field, whether it was sport, art, computer sciences or other fields of endeavour. If we consider what this means in bridge terms, a player needs to play for roughly twenty hours a week for ten years to achieve a high level of knowledge and expertise. However, there is a caveat here—playing for 10,000 hours doesn't mean you will be a world class player or even an expert player. Just as not everyone is athletic enough to become a champion tennis player or golfer, it's the same in bridge—not everyone will be world class or even expert just because they did 10,000 hours of practice. After achieving a certain level of expertise over time, a bridge player's skill level is limited by their individual ability.

This concept is roughly depicted in the chart shown on the next page. The bottom, middle and top lines show the respective learning curves for club, national and international level players.

In the **learning phase**, improvement happens relatively quickly as basic bidding, defence, play techniques and other aspects of bridge are acquired. For a player who will eventually become an international level player, the rate of improvement is faster than for one whose final level will be in club bridge.

In the **development phase**, the rate of improvement slows as more complex techniques such as endplays, squeezes and advanced bidding skills are acquired.

In the **performance phase**, players are utilising all their knowledge and acquired skills. There is less scope for improvement from skill acquisition and performance is reliant on other factors such as concentration, making the right decisions at critical times in the match, keeping calm under pressure and so on. In this phase, the difference between players who have reached the performance phase is attributed to their ability to implement these other factors. A club level player who has strong concentration is more likely to beat another club level player whose attention wanders, even if their other skills are equivalent.

A player will reach their optimum performance level after working on

Skill Development – Maximum level limited by player ability

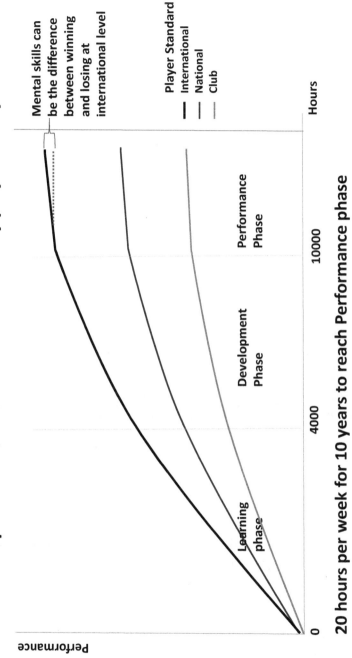

Mental skills can be the difference between winning and losing at international level

Player Standard
— International
— National
— Club

Performance

Learning phase

Development Phase

Performance Phase

0   4000   10000   Hours

20 hours per week for 10 years to reach Performance phase

their game for thousands of hours, but that level will be limited by their innate ability. The higher one's innate 'ability', the higher the end skill level.

So, what is the difference between a player who wins and one who loses, where the players have had roughly the same number of hours of training and both have acquired the same amount of ability and possess the same level of expertise? Experts now generally agree that the answer to this question lies in how good players are at a number of factors *beyond their ability* at their sport/technical activity. One of these factors is mental skills.

Sportspeople have used sports psychology to help them with the mental side of the game for many years with its use becoming more widespread from the mid-1970's. There are certainly some instances of earlier use than this, but I don't believe there was a formalised, widespread and structured approach before that time. Certainly, there wasn't the wealth of knowledge there is today. Yet despite bridge's huge mental components, I have found little documentation on using sports psychology in bridge. Perhaps the best players are already using the techniques described in this book and the rest of the bridge world is left in the dark? However, it seems unlikely that many players are using mental tools given the lack of published information or public discussion on the topic.

This book will give players of all levels a mental toolbox—i.e. a set of mental skills that can help them with their game in the variety of situations that are thrust upon them in competitive bridge. Just as we have a range of system conventions or card-play techniques that we draw on in competition, each of us should also have a number of mental 'tools' to assist us with achieving the best performance level possible within the limits of our technical ability.

These mental skills include:

» the ability to relax when under pressure;

» rehearsal techniques to improve your play;

» the ability to maintain concentration and focus;

» pre-match preparation; and

» match management.

If you are a player who gets off to a bad start in tournaments or who struggles to win in tournaments when you are leading or who loses concentration or gets nervous or loses your cool—mental tools can help you. Understanding how to improve your mental skills and gaining the necessary skills in this area will assist players of all levels to maximise their potential at bridge and get the most out of the game.

Chapter 2

Be Ready for The Kick-Off

"Are you nervous?"

When I competed in my first Commonwealth Games as a shooter, all of the Australian team members received lots of letters from schoolkids in support of our quest to win 'gold'. One of the most common questions from the kids was "Are you nervous?". The answer is a definite yes— everyone gets a little bit nervous but some people deal with it better than others.

'Opening round nerves' are as much an issue in the bridge world as they are in competitive sport and other fields of endeavour. In tennis we often see good players who are the clear favourites to win a match drop their serve in the opening game. In golf, great players will frequently make a wild tee shot on the first hole. In football, players often fumble at the first bounce or miss their first shot at goal in a match. Many sportspeople suffer from nerves at the start of a match and this nervousness is commonly attributed to match pressure. Over and over again in sport, we see very good athletes lose a race or match after having made an error in the early stages of their competition from which it is impossible to recover. This is particularly true in 'target' sports like shooting, golf, archery and so on, but other events such as cycling, swimming, athletics and gymnastics are not immune from this phenomenon.

A number of factors can contribute to this phenomenon but the most obvious is anxiety which affects the athlete's ability to perform at their normal level. The athlete afflicted by anxiety at the beginning of an event (or during an event) will often make a costly mistake from which recovery is impossible. They finish below their best, pondering what might have been if they hadn't messed up their start or that shot or that jump or that bid.

I have observed the phenomenon of first-round nerves quite often in bridge where an otherwise competent player will completely misplay or misbid a board or two in their opening match and turn a potential win into a loss. While many factors play a part, it seems clear that first-round nerves are one of the factors affecting performance in the bridge world, just as they affect performers in other sports and activities.

Several years ago, I was playing in a national event. My partner was a player with many years of experience and was generally considered to be a competent player. Nevertheless, in the first round, my partner in the South seat failed to take the opportunity presented to her to make an unmakeable contract. Her hands were visibly shaking as she played the first board of the match where South became declarer in five clubs:

Dealer: South
Vulnerable: None

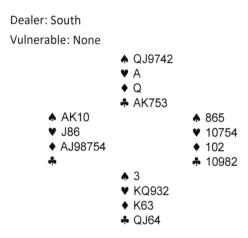

West kicked off by leading the ace of spades, cashed the ace of diamonds and after much thought continued with a low spade won by dummy's queen. Game is now easily made given that spades are 3-3 by ruffing a spade to hand (establishing the whole suit) before drawing trumps.

There is good reason to think that West has the remaining spade honour, given East's failure to attempt to take the setting trick. My partner took a line that failed when she continued at trick four by unblocking the ace of hearts and drawing three rounds of trumps by playing ace of clubs, then three of clubs to declarer's queen, followed by the jack leaving this layout:

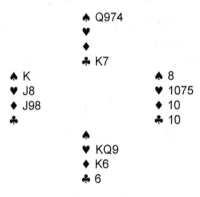

```
              ♠ Q974
              ♥
              ♦
              ♣ K7
  ♠ K                      ♠ 8
  ♥ J8                     ♥ 1075
  ♦ J98                    ♦ 10
  ♣                        ♣ 10
              ♠
              ♥ KQ9
              ♦ K6
              ♣ 6
```

Declarer continued with the king of diamonds and tried to ruff a diamond, which was overruffed by East for one down.

Perhaps declarer placed West with ace doubleton in spades and was worried about an overruff if she chose to ruff out the spade suit. This is hardly realistic! How could East have ducked the king of spades when this could easily have been the setting trick? Regardless, simply cashing one round of clubs would have revealed the trump situation and clarified the layout, leading to the winning play.

The contract can now be made by ruffing a spade. Seeing the even split in spades, you clear trumps and then cross to dummy to enjoy all your winning spades which West, who may have been afflicted by some nerves herself, has so kindly set up for you.

Our opponents were a well-established pair who have won national events and this may have added to the pressure my partner felt on this hand. It is hard to know what was going through declarer's mind at the time. However, it seems more likely to have been a case of the first-round nerves which many experience, rather than a lack of skill necessary to make the correct play when presented with the opportunity.

Whatever the reason, after being given a golden opportunity by the opponents, my partner took a line that failed whereas in a more relaxed environment at her local club, I expect she would have got it right every time. One off and the loss of what would have been a ten-IMP gain for making the game wasn't a great way to build a confident start to the tournament. While it's not impossible to recover from an early loss in the tournament, it is so much better if you don't have to.

Are nerves bad then?

Almost everyone gets a bit nervous at the start of an event. Some people have an impression that nerves are bad, but nervousness isn't always a negative thing and it doesn't always adversely affect performance. A little bit of nervousness generates increased arousal and some arousal is necessary for optimum performance. There are many positives to be gained from the increased stimulation of the central nervous system that comes from heightened arousal. These advantages include enhanced awareness, visual acuity, increased cognitive awareness and so on.

Issues arise when a player's nervousness is so great that the arousal level becomes too high and passes the optimal arousal point. This creates an overly anxious state (see 'Arousal and Performance diagram' on the following page). In this state, performance may suffer because when the level of arousal or stress is too high, the result is a negative effect on cognitive processes such as attention, memory and problem solving. In bridge terms, being a little anxious can be helpful since being more alert and 'switched on' can improve performance but being too anxious leads to a drop-off in performance as the player struggles to think clearly when faced with a difficult choice.

Players who know that nerves have had a detrimental impact on their performance need techniques to help, just as we have system agreements

Arousal and Performance

The relationship between arousal and performance was first investigated by psychologists Robert M. Yerkes and John Dillingham Dodson in 1908. The chart below is a commonly shown depiction of Yerkes - Dodson Law[1]. The law dictates that performance increases with physiological or mental arousal, but only up to a point. When levels of arousal become too high, performance decreases, particularly if performing complex or difficult tasks such as playing bridge.

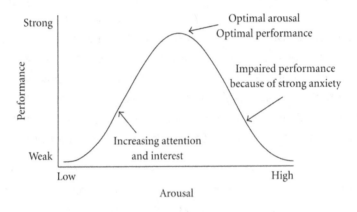

Figure 1: Hebbian variation of Yerkes Dodson Law

1   Yerkes RM, Dodson JD (1908). 'The relation of strength of stimulus to rapidity of habit-formation'. Journal of Comparative Neurology and Psychology. 18: 459–482. doi:10.1002/cne.920180503

to deal with different circumstances on the hands we are dealt. Using these mental techniques will help to ensure we don't allow nerves at the start or at any time through the match to lead to lower than desired results. Let's consider some of these techniques.

Be ready to play by warming up

While there are many techniques to help competitors relax and deal with nervous tension and match anxiety, a good first step is to be ready to go on the first board with good match preparation. Match preparation will assist you in getting off to a good start, whether it is at a major tournament or simply your local game at the club.

In sport, players know what to expect at the start of the match or race and it is possible to make practicing starts very close to reality. For example, a runner can quite easily practice starting races. Athletes generally spend many hours practicing this aspect to ensure they get a good start to their competition. When I was training for my shooting events, practicing starting matches included pre-match warm-up and preparation before every training session and match. It is therefore surprising to me that many bridge players will enter the competition 'cold' in sporting terms.

Most of us will have experienced starting a tournament with a complicated hand at board one. If you aren't prepared and haven't got your mind into gear, you can easily make a basic error. Before you know it you've gone off in, or failed to bid, a game or slam you could have made! How annoying to lose IMPs to a mistake that is easily overcome by good preparation. It is impossible to predict the hand you will get on board one, but you can manage all the other aspects to ensure you are prepared and in the right frame of mind for 'the kick-off'.

This next deal, while not exceptionally tricky, was from the opening match of one of Australia's largest events. It was the first board of the round. I was playing with a new partner and I was one of only four pairs in the 200+ strong field playing in six no-trumps after partner sitting North opened one diamond (although a few pairs did find slam in spades and diamonds).

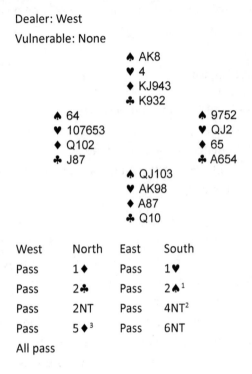

Dealer: West

Vulnerable: None

```
                        ♠ AK8
                        ♥ 4
                        ♦ KJ943
                        ♣ K932
        ♠ 64                            ♠ 9752
        ♥ 107653                        ♥ QJ2
        ♦ Q102                          ♦ 65
        ♣ J87                           ♣ A654
                        ♠ QJ103
                        ♥ AK98
                        ♦ A87
                        ♣ Q10
```

West	North	East	South
Pass	1♦	Pass	1♥
Pass	2♣	Pass	2♠[1]
Pass	2NT	Pass	4NT[2]
Pass	5♦[3]	Pass	6NT
All pass			

1 - 4th suit forcing to game

2 - Quantitative

3 - One ace and happy to go on

West led the seven of hearts. When dummy came down, I could see that six no-trumps was not an amazing contract requiring diamonds to be brought in for five tricks. In this situation, a few things are going on with the player's mental state:

» playing the first board of an event generally creates an increased level of anxiety on its own; and,

» playing with a new partner might make one feel slightly more anxious or nervous; and,

» reaching a dicey slam on the first board of the match increases the level of anxiety that a player feels; and,

» if your opponents are a pair who have defeated you previously, or who are a pair you know, you may also be feeling under increased pressure to perform.

In this state of mind, players are more likely to make simple errors that cost heavily. Since my pre-match routine includes a warm-up before the start of play, I kept calm and played the diamonds in the best way—cashing the diamond ace and finessing the jack on the second round—to land the slam.

To play well from the outset, bridge players can increase their chances of success by warming up, both mentally and physically, in the same way that professional athletes warm up before their events. It is hard to imagine an athlete at the Olympic Games walking out on to the field of play without having done a warm-up, yet bridge players often go straight from the breakfast room or from the bedroom to the playing room without touching a card. Waking up the mind and body before you start your bridge tournament can also help with the early match nerves that some players experience. If you walk in for the first round having warmed up properly, then you are more likely to play at your desired level than if you are mentally 'cold'.

We would all like the opportunity to work our way into the tournament with some straightforward contracts on the first few boards, but often that isn't what happens. Being 'ready to play' from board one is critical to success as you don't want to be playing catch-up. Being a feared opponent is far better than being someone who picks up a reputation for struggling when the pressure is on, or who always loses in the first round. Why give your opponents an edge when you don't have to?

Warming up for bridge comprises two parts—waking up the body physically by waking up the central nervous system and waking up the mind.

Wake up the body's central nervous system

You don't have to do anything particularly athletic to wake up your body's central nervous system. Our brain needs oxygen to function properly and to be mentally alert, so activating your body physically will help to wake up the central nervous system. There are a few very simple and low impact ways to wake up the central nervous system, get the blood flowing and physically wake up the body. These include walking, yoga or stretching in your hotel room, having a swim or similar activity. You can do more vigorous exercise if you are younger and/or fitter, but for many bridge players a 15-20 minute walk before or after breakfast is enough to help wake up the body and get ready for action. Participating in physical activity also has a lasting effect after its conclusion, especially if it is performed regularly.

Since bridge events are often broken into morning and afternoon sessions, it is also worth refraining from a heavy lunch which tends to draw the blood to the stomach and make you drowsy in the session immediately after lunch. If you make going for a 5-10 minute walk during the lunch break before the afternoon session part of your routine, it will also help get your oxygen flowing and allow you to return to the table ready to play.

Wake up the mind

Waking up the mind may be managed in many ways. What works for one pair or player might not be effective for another. Like all areas of improvement, each player must experiment to find out what works best for them and their partner/teammates, but the point is to become mentally alert before the first round. Juggling is often used by athletes—both for waking up the mind and for eye-hand co-ordination. This might also be effective for bridge players, but not everyone has the dexterity to manage it, so here are a few other more bridge-related ideas on waking up your mind before your first session.

» Have a hand record(s) from a recent competition and plan your bidding and/or play on about half a dozen hands.

» Play a few hands of bridge, if you can find some other willing participants, or online/against the computer if you can't. Remember this is a warm-up designed to get your mind in gear, so a few hands are enough!

» Do a few problems from a bridge book suitable for your skill level.

» Do a crossword puzzle, sudoku or other mind game.

One of the effects of this mental wake-up routine will be that you can make a mistake in your hotel room before play, cost-free, rather than at the table in the first match! In one of my partnerships we found that playing for about twenty minutes on Bridge Base Online (BBO) around an hour and a half before the start of the day's play really helped us to be ready to play, particularly on the first day of a tournament.

Our warm-up paid early dividends when this next deal hit the table in the first match of the day. My partner was on the ball and took an action which encouraged our opponents to take a poor line in four spades.

Dealer: East

Vulnerable: N-S

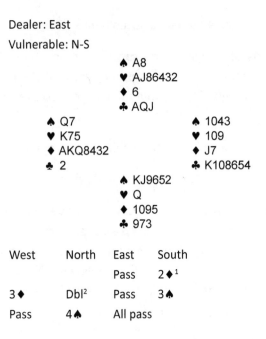

	♠ A8		
	♥ AJ86432		
	♦ 6		
	♣ AQJ		
♠ Q7		♠ 1043	
♥ K75		♥ 109	
♦ AKQ8432		♦ J7	
♣ 2		♣ K108654	
	♠ KJ9652		
	♥ Q		
	♦ 1095		
	♣ 973		

West	North	East	South
		Pass	2♦¹
3♦	Dbl²	Pass	3♠
Pass	4♠	All pass	

1 - Weak 2 in either major, or 21 - 22 balanced

2 - Strong inquiry after interference

My partner sitting West led the ace of diamonds on which I gave upside-down count with the seven. On seeing dummy, West took the unusual action of switching to the seven of spades. After much thought declarer won with the ace and took the spade finesse to what was now West's singleton queen. West continued with the king and queen of diamonds for one off and ten IMPs to our side.

South chose a line of play without properly considering what could go wrong—i.e. what happens if the spade finesse fails. While this was an important event, and it is possible South was feeling the pressure, it is equally possible that South had not warmed up mentally before the start of play. Her mind was not yet 'tuned in' at the bridge table.

Warming up to enable you to perform at your optimum level from the outset of an event will help you to make the right decisions at the table from the very first bid you make or card you play.

Give your body some 'fuel'

I was surprised recently when a young player told me that he doesn't normally eat breakfast and often not lunch when playing a bridge competition. At the time we were discussing some strategies to overcome anxiety at the start of tournaments which he had reported feeling. One of my suggestions to help overcome this was that he tries eating something healthy for breakfast such as a low GI food like porridge, eggs and wholegrain toast, or similar. A bridge tournament is a bit of a marathon and your body and brain need energy to function. You don't want to eat so much that you feel like you need a nap, but I believe some food is a must to help maintain energy and concentration throughout the event. More on nutrition for bridge in chapter ten (refer page 166).

Have a routine at the tournament

Anyone who has ever watched tennis, golf or other elite sports will have seen how athletes go through their final preparation before starting play. Rafael Nadal (tennis) always takes the same approach before serving or receiving a ball. Karrie Webb (golf) takes a short swing every time before setting up to hit a drive on the golf tee. Ralf Schumann (multiple World and Olympic champion rapid-fire shooter) was like a robot with his precision of routine in preparing for each course of fire. All of these athletes are multiple world champions and major event winners, not just because of their natural ability, their skill and capacity to execute their technique flawlessly, but because of their consistent approach to every shot and every competition.

Like these athletes, it is important for bridge players to have a routine before play, as this gets your mind into its 'competition' zone. Doing the same thing every time will help ensure we reach our 'match ready' state for the first board. I had a match day routine for my shooting competitions and I also had an equipment checklist to make sure I remembered everything I was supposed to pack for the event. It isn't much use arriving at the competition only to find that you have left a critical piece of equipment at home several hours travel away. In fact, at an overseas event at which I competed a German shooter did just that and his coach had to spend eight hours driving home and back to collect the missing piece in time for the next day's competition!

Similarly, for bridge it is an important part of preparation to be ready when play starts. Remember to check what time play begins and get to the table on time. Find out what time the restart is after lunch or breaks before you leave the playing area. Have your system card, pen, water bottle, headache tablets, or whatever else you normally require with you. Get to the table early enough to give yourself some time to review the opponents' system. The point here is to create a consistent environment that enables you (and your partner) to perform at your best—not one where you or your partner are stressed out before you even play a card. A bridge competition checklist is included at the end of this chapter—feel free to add to this for your own requirements.

Having a routine before play will also assist you with taking the right approach when faced with hands like this next one early in your round where you need to make the right decisions in bidding and play:

Dealer: North

Vulnerable: N-S

```
                    ♠ A
                    ♥ KQ74
                    ♦ KJ87
                    ♣ AQ62
        ♠ K5                     ♠ 1098643
        ♥ 1063                   ♥ 8
        ♦ 1094                   ♦ Q632
        ♣ J9854                  ♣ K7
                    ♠ QJ72
                    ♥ AJ952
                    ♦ A5
                    ♣ 103
```

West	North	East	South
	1♣¹	Pass	1♦²
Pass	2♠³	Pass	2NT⁴
Pass	3♣⁵	Pass	4♥⁶
Pass	5♦⁷	Pass	6♥
All Pass			

1 - Minimum of one

2 - Four or more hearts

3 - Heart support, 0 or 1 spade and invitational to game or slam

4 - Keycard

5 - 0 or 3 keycards

6 - Signoff if zero keycards

7 - Three keycards, the queen of trumps and the king of diamonds

Our side reached slam in hearts after an accurate bidding sequence. West led the ten of diamonds. On seeing dummy, I thought that despite all the points there was still a fair amount of work to do. After winning with dummy's king, I cashed the king of hearts and the ace of spades before playing a low heart over to my jack. Next I tried a low spade. When West played the king, I ruffed in dummy and drew the outstanding trump. I crossed back to hand with a diamond to the ace and tried the club finesse for an overtrick, but it lost to the king.

This is one of those hands that often cause problems for me with so many viable lines to choose from to make the contract. Here my routine now is to slow down and think about the play for quite a while before playing to trick one. Additionally, having a routine before the play of each board will also assist with achieving consistent results. I discuss this aspect in detail in chapter four. On this hand following my routine allowed me to focus on the task at hand and come up with a winning line.

Experiment to find out what works for you

Good preparation is a key part of mental management. Utilising the techniques in this chapter will assist in getting you off to a good start at your next tournament 'kick-off'.

There is no simple answer to getting off to a good start. No single thing is likely to solve all the problems you might be having in this area. Each of us operates differently and each of us must test what will work best for us by trial and error. The key is to try a variety of different things and once you have identified the best approach for you, stick to it.

One final thought—don't forget to bring your confidence with you. If you approach each match with a positive attitude, you are more likely to have a better result. This brings me to the topic of my next chapter—how to stay positive.

Bridge Competition Checklist

Making sure you arrive at the table 'ready to play' will ensure you give yourself the best chance to perform. Below is a simple checklist to help you be ready:

- Know the start time for each session – don't assume or guess it will always be the same each day
- System cards (four – since you might lose some!)
- System notes
- Personal scoresheet/scorebook
- Pen (bring one for your partner too in case they forget!)
- Water/drink bottle
- Headache tablets or any other medicine you need
- Spectacles (the correct ones)
- Mints or snack bars
- Sweater/jacket in case the room is too cold for you. Consider your clothing in general and whether you are likely to be too warm.

Chapter 3

Positive Mindsets

"Oh no, you're here! We'll all be competing for second now!"

– anonymous competitor

When I picked up this hand as North, I wanted to be in game and thought slam might be a possibility. Then the bidding started:

Dealer: West
Vulnerable: N-S

```
                    ♠ AKJ3
                    ♥ AKJ8642
                    ♦ 2
                    ♣ 9
        ♠ Q987                      ♠ 542
        ♥ Q                         ♥ 7
        ♦ K74                       ♦ AQ109853
        ♣ AJ1087                    ♣ Q3
                    ♠ 106
                    ♥ 10953
                    ♦ J6
                    ♣ K6542
```

West	North	East	South
1♣	Dbl	Rdbl[1]	1♥
1♠	4♥[2]	5♦	Pass
Pass	5♥	All Pass	

1 - Normally 10+HCP

2 - I can't believe my partner has hearts!

Once West opened in front of me and East redoubled, slam didn't seem likely. However, after partner bid hearts and East bid five diamonds, bidding five hearts vulnerable against not when partner could have a yarborough still seemed a good choice. West's spade bid and East's redouble seemed to mark partner with a spade shortage. Sure enough, eleven tricks rolled home after the defenders cashed the two minor suit aces. Getting a 'five-level' decision right is always challenging. When it pays off, it is a big confidence boost, particularly when it happens early in a match.

Having the right mental approach, remaining positive and thinking clearly about the inferences from the bidding and the options on the hand are important skills at the bridge table. On the above hand, it would have been easy to ride an emotional roller-coaster through the hand: "Wow, what a hand! Oh, the opponents have opened...that's disappointing. And now they've redoubled! Wait, partner bid my seven-card suit?" but the final decision to bid 'five over five' had to be based on logic, not emotions.

Self-fulfilling prophesies

Several years ago, I was having a particularly good season in shooting. This was before I had made my first national shooting team, but I had been successful at various events in my state before that time. Prior to the start of the season I had had some work done on my equipment and my first competition in the new year brought success. I went on to win almost every event I entered in that season. I recall arriving at a competition venue late in the year to be greeted by an opponent with the comment "Oh no you're here, we'll all be competing for second now!".

At the time I was astonished that someone would even think such a thing, let alone say it out loud to a competitor. Even though at the time I was not as knowledgeable about sports psychology as now, I would never have said anything like that, even to myself. I certainly wouldn't have said that to an opponent.

Like bridge, shooting is a sport often won by very small margins—one or two points can be the difference between first and tenth. With opponents who had an attitude like that, is it any surprise I won the event? Even though I had been having a great season and would have been one of the favourites to win, the comment showed this competitor—who would have been in with a chance at winning—had pretty much given up mentally before the first shot was fired!

It seems this type of attitude is alive and well at the bridge table. At one competition at my local club, my partner and I sat down to play against a pair and were greeted with a comment like "Oh no, not you! Don't beat us up by too much." It is a bit of a self-fulfilling prophesy, don't you think? The players think they are going to get beaten by us. No surprise when they do. Certainly, when players say something like that to me, my confidence gets a boost and I think I have an edge.

I am sure we have all seen and heard examples of pairs going into a match with a less than optimistic mindset. I have heard players say things like: "We've drawn the top seed in round one!" or "We are playing against those guys and they are going to slaughter us," and so on. Going in with this mindset means you aren't really surprised when you lose—after all, you expected to lose, didn't you? In fact, you have even given yourself permission to lose by having such a negative mindset.

Approach each event with a positive attitude

While there is no substitute for strong technical skills and ability, when these are roughly equal, success in competition is brought about by confidence and the mental approach you bring to the game. If you sit down expecting to lose, then you are already putting a sub-conscious weight on your shoulders. A player who approaches a match with a strong mental attitude will be more likely to make the right decisions, and in the long run be more successful, than a player expressing negative sentiments. The negativity might be about the opponents, the system they play, a convention they play, the signalling they use and so on. It doesn't matter whether you verbalise the sentiment, or whether you just think it—the effect will be the same on your confidence. Consider this deal:

Dealer: East
Vulnerable: None

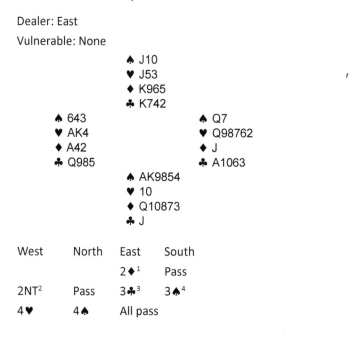

```
                    ♠ J10
                    ♥ J53
                    ♦ K965
                    ♣ K742
    ♠ 643                       ♠ Q7
    ♥ AK4                       ♥ Q98762
    ♦ A42                       ♦ J
    ♣ Q985                      ♣ A1063
                    ♠ AK9854
                    ♥ 10
                    ♦ Q10873
                    ♣ J
```

West	North	East	South
		2♦¹	Pass
2NT²	Pass	3♣³	3♠⁴
4♥	4♠	All pass	

1 - Multi 2♦ showing a weak six card major or 20 - 22 balanced

2 - Forcing enquiry

3 - Good weak two in hearts

4 - Lead directing for partner—wish I'd bid the first time!

My partner propelled me to game after my lead directing overcall. He later commented he couldn't fathom what type of hand I would have that allowed me to pass at the two level and enter the bidding at the three level. At the time I considered my hand a bit weak for a direct overcall at the two level over what might be a pre-emptive hand, but after the two no-trump strong enquiry from West, I wanted to make a bid that would be lead directing and suggest a sacrifice over a potential four heart contract. On reflection I think an immediate two spade overcall is better with the distributional values in the hand.

It was surprising to me that West didn't double, given that East, who had shown a 'good' weak two in hearts, must have had some values outside the heart suit. West led the ace of hearts. From my point of view, it seemed likely that East was going to be short in diamonds, and so I focussed on willing West to continue with hearts. Eventually she did and now I was able to wrap up ten tricks when the trumps split favourably.

Clearly, a heart continuation isn't right here. West stated after the hand that she was unsure about which suit to switch to (her partner's heart card should have signalled a club) and she thought the heart continuation was 'safe'. It is clear on this hand that after a club switch, East would have immediately switched to the jack of diamonds. West would be likely to recognise this as a singleton and give East a diamond ruff for one off. Incidentally, on the lie of the cards five hearts makes, but the line to achieving that contract requires precise play so defeating four spades would have been a good result for East-West.

Frankly, telling the opponents you didn't know what to do on a hand doesn't help your or your partner's confidence at all. It just helps the opponents with theirs! It would have been far better for this player to have discussed what could have been done differently at the end of the round, or even at the end of the tournament. Good players will know they got a gift from the defence. There is no need to help them even more by telling them that you don't know what you are doing!

Positive thinking doesn't always work so nicely, but it can't hurt. Sitting quietly and confidently at the table while the opponents try and work out what to do will go a long way to improving your results at the table.

Playing against the guest speaker!

Early in my bridge career I was playing at a large national event. Because I didn't have that many masterpoints at the time, I invariably found myself playing against top seeded pairs/teams in the early rounds, most of whom I knew nothing about. This was probably a blessing in disguise as it meant that I wasn't immediately intimidated by the opponents. As bridge seeding is often based on the number of masterpoints a pair or team holds, this number can sometimes have more to do with years of play rather than ability. Consequently, the pair's seeding isn't always a true reflection of ability. However, in this case the pair we were up against was the late Ted Chadwick (one of Australia's all-time best players), playing professionally with his regular sponsor. I sat down at the table and introduced myself to the opponents who did the same. As this was round one, the tournament organiser stood up and made a few announcements, one of which was that the guest speaker at Friday's lecture would be Ted Chadwick. Wow! As if we didn't have enough to intimidate us already playing a more highly-ranked pair—we got the guest speaker as well!

It turned out that we had a good set against this pair, losing the match more because they bid all their games in a round that was clearly their way, rather than because of anything we did. At the end of the round Ted graciously complimented us on our play. Nevertheless, one hand stuck in my memory from this match:

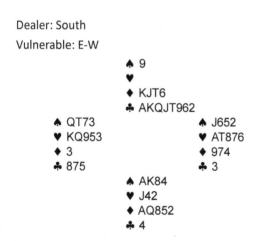

On the deal above we had the methods to enable us to bid the North-South grand slam in either clubs or diamonds. However, I was still an inexperienced player who invariably made lots of mistakes and we were playing some system methods which I had clearly misunderstood when they were explained to me. While our methods were good enough in theory, I made a bidding error and turned what would have been a nice pick-up into a small loss on the hand when I couldn't find out which specific aces my partner held. Clearly the importance of knowing your system well was a key lesson learnt from this experience, but also knowing that I could be competitive with 'good' players was a big confidence boost for me in the early stages of my bridge journey.

So, a first step in approaching a competition is to have a positive mindset. The point here is really about believing in yourself. Sure, the opponents might have a superior record and be more highly ranked than you, but that is no reason to give up hope. In this round, we held our own against a stronger pair. We ended the tournament quite well placed because we didn't give up on a match simply because the cards were running against us or because our opponents had a higher seeding number or because one of us made an error.

We also didn't give the opponents a boost by making a negative remark about how we were going to perform against them, or 'to go easy on us'. Despite losing the match, our good performance gave me a lot of confidence for this and future tournaments. Believing in your own abilities and trusting that you are good enough to win against strong players is a critical step to achieving success at the bridge table.

Belief only helps if it is founded upon realistic thoughts— i.e. it needs to be believable. My thoughts about playing strong pairs, particularly early in an event, can be summed up as follows:

» They get 13 cards each, the same as my partner and I do;

» I've drawn them in the first round which is good, because they might not have got their act together, particularly if it is a while since they last played together;

» They are usually really nice at the table, and often go out of their way to help less experienced players understand the meaning of the bidding in their auctions;

» I might learn something from them that will improve my own bridge, especially if I take the opportunity to ask them about a hand after the round;

» I like playing good pairs because their bidding and carding is often more reliable than weaker pairs, unless of course they are trying to be devious; and

» If their team is 'supposed' to beat ours, an early good result by us might upset their confidence.

Consequently, when I sat down to play against Ted and heard he was the guest speaker, I thought how great it was that I got to play against such a good player. I was excited by the opportunity it presented. I didn't think about getting thrashed or failing or anything negative.

When you give your opponents a confidence boost, by making—or even thinking—overtly negative statements, you are also giving yourself a handicap. It is hard enough to win without boosting your opponents' confidence. Keeping this type of attitude will assist you greatly when you pick up a hand like this against good opponents:

Dealer: South

Vulnerable: All

```
                        ♠ 3
                        ♥ A1097
                        ♦ K862
                        ♣ AKQ4
        ♠ K10842                        ♠ J7
        ♥ K32                           ♥ QJ
        ♦ AQJ                           ♦ 754
        ♣ 92                            ♣ J108653
                        ♠ AQ965
                        ♥ 8654
                        ♦ 1093
                        ♣ 7
```

West	North	East	South
			Pass
1♠	Dbl	Pass	2♥[1]
Pass	3♥[2]	Pass	4♥
All Pass			

1 - Choosing two hearts over pass or one no-trump.

2 - Invitational, showing extras

The decision whether to pass one spade doubled or show a possible heart fit wasn't easy for me in the South seat. From my perspective there wasn't a guarantee that North-South can even make four hearts while defeating one spade doubled might deliver the par result on the board. Partner is also not guaranteed to hold four hearts. Choosing to compete for a part-score rather than seeking a penalty from a doubled part-score contract is never an obvious decision. The relatively weak texture in the spades together with being under the opening spade bidder might persuade one not to pass the double on this hand. Hence, on this occasion I elected to show my hearts and was encouraged to bid game by my partner's invitation.

West led the nine of clubs. When dummy came down, I could see four hearts was going to require a lot of work and good timing, although I could also see the contract had a reasonable prospect of making. I won the club lead with dummy's ace and continued with the king, pitching a diamond from my hand. I now played a spade to my ace and led the ten of diamonds towards dummy's king with West contributing the queen.

After winning the diamond in dummy, I continued with dummy's queen of clubs, discarding a spade from my hand while West ruffed. West continued with the eight of spades to East's jack and my queen as I pitched the last club from dummy. A low heart to dummy's ace, followed by another heart dropping East-West's queen and king of hearts, and the contract was made.

It would have been easy for me to be negative on this type of hand or to second-guess the decision I made at the table to bid hearts rather than no-trumps or passing for a penalty double of the spade part-score. Nevertheless, once the decision has been made it is important to focus on the task at hand rather than any consideration of whether the decision made was the correct one. This will ensure you play the hand to give yourself the best opportunity to make the contract. Any extraneous thoughts are simply a distraction which might lead to an unintentional error.

Beating your 'nemesis'

Clearly, not all pairs sit down expecting to get beaten by the opponents or make overtly negative statements. Sometimes subconsciously we develop doubts about our ability to win a match. For example, there are often pairs you play against regularly in competition whom you and your partner struggle to do well against. It might be the system they play, their attitude at the table, their demeanour or a host of other factors that just niggle you. It can even be due to nothing other than your poor playing record against them.

In a game where luck occasionally plays a role, over time you will inevitably end up doing well against some opponents and poorly against others simply by luck of the draw and natural variance. Over time the consistently 'less than optimal' performances you have against a pair can add up mentally and reach the point where you enter your matches against those opponents with some doubts in your mind about your ability to beat them.

In cases where you come up against players against whom you have a poor record or against whom you lost the last time you played them, it is important to have some positive statements handy to enable you to change the paradigm and perform well against the pair. A simple mental thought statement like "We beat pair X, and pair X thrashed these two so we can beat them too" when you sit down to play will help build your confidence and even up the contest.

In sport, as well as in life, we often hear about people talking about the power of positive thinking. This is a critical aspect of mental management in sport, and inherent in this concept is the following:

'The more you think about, talk about and write about something happening the more likely it is to come true.'[1]

The opponents who sit down to play thinking they are going to get beaten or remembering the last time a pair beat them or who are intimidated by the ranking of their opponents or their system, etc., have entered the match with the wrong mindset. Even if their skill level is sufficient to allow them to win, it is highly unlikely they will be able to succeed if they approach the match with the wrong mental attitude.

Use Positive Affirmations

Closely aligned with the idea of positive self-talk at the event is the use of positive affirmations before the event. Sportspeople, people in business and people in all walks of life use positive affirmations to help them

---

1   L. Bassham: With Winning in Mind; 1988; P47

succeed. There is a lot of literature on the power of positive thinking and similar. There are hundreds of examples from sports people who have used positive affirmations in their self-talk to help them believe they can win. Take this deal:

Dealer: East

Vulnerable: N-S

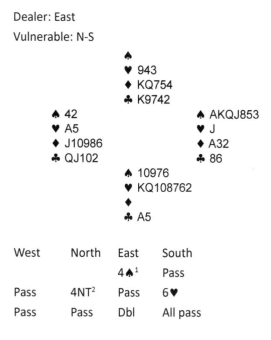

	♠	
	♥ 943	
	♦ KQ754	
	♣ K9742	

♠ 42		♠ AKQJ853
♥ A5		♥ J
♦ J10986		♦ A32
♣ QJ102		♣ 86

	♠ 10976	
	♥ KQ108762	
	♦	
	♣ A5	

West	North	East	South
		4♠[1]	Pass
Pass	4NT[2]	Pass	6♥
Pass	Pass	Dbl	All pass

1 - By agreement, strong (8+ playing tricks).

2 - Take-out; usually showing two places to play

East's double of six hearts with two aces was not unreasonable although an expectation that the ace of spades would take a trick may have been optimistic. On the lead of the four of spades my partner's hand came down. I must confess that my first thought was not a very positive one! Even those most practiced at mental management occasionally have a lapse and something along the lines of 'you bid four no-trumps with that pile of junk?' went through my mind. Allowing that thought to remain would not have been correct and so I re-focussed on the task at hand with my cue word (see page 72). I thought about what needed to happen to make the slam after the spade lead and I then proceeded to play for that layout.

(hand repeated below)

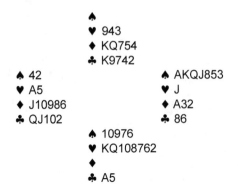

After ruffing the spade lead in dummy, I immediately took the ruffing finesse in diamonds by playing the king of diamonds, covered by the ace and ruffed in hand. I ruffed a second spade in dummy and then pitched my third spade on the queen of diamonds before ruffing a diamond back to hand. For the contract to make, I decided that West had to have the ace of hearts and not the jack so I played my last spade hoping to ruff with the nine of hearts.[2] When West pitched a diamond on the spade, I knew I was home. I returned to hand with a club to the ace and played the king of hearts. West rose with the ace, and the jack of hearts fell. I won the diamond return, drew the last trump and claimed.

On this deal I was lucky East-West didn't find the only lead to defeat the slam—the ace of hearts and another heart. There was clearly some luck at play here since making a slam missing three aces is not an everyday occurrence. When something like this happens, it certainly gives a big boost to one's confidence. However, more important is the attitude you

2   Note that you can also make the contract without relying on West not having the jack of hearts by drawing trumps after ruffing a diamond back to hand. Given the 4♠ opening, East is unlikely to have any more diamonds left (and has already shown up with 7 spades, 1+ hearts [by assumption] and 3 diamonds so can't hold more than two clubs). If West is the sole owner of the diamond suit, you can draw trumps and run hearts to squeeze West in the minors, which is what happens using this line.

take on the hand when partner's dummy isn't quite what you imagined when you made your bid. The "how can I make this" thought must be in your mind as opposed to the "how do I avoid going for a big number here" thought, or even worse, "how could my partner bid that way?".

I used positive thought to great effect when I was competing in shooting. At the time I had won two gold medals in major international competitions for pairs events, but I had never won the individual medal in a major event. As I planned my approach for what would be my third Commonwealth Games—the 2002 games in Manchester—which also might have been my last chance for individual glory as an ageing athlete, I really wanted to win the individual medal. It may sound arrogant, but I never considered the possibility I would fail at the selection trials—I knew I was the favourite to win the trials and qualify. At that time, I had been one of the leading female shooters for several years in Australia, almost always in the top two or three in each competition. It was unthinkable to me that I wouldn't qualify.

I had always dismissed the idea of making positive affirmations as 'not for me'. It wasn't necessarily that I didn't believe they would work, but rather I just didn't see them as something that I needed. Nevertheless as 2002 approached and trials loomed on the horizon, I decided that making and using a positive affirmation couldn't do any harm. I kept a training diary in which I recorded all my training and competition performances, notes about technique and so on. So, I wrote in my training diary at every session for about one year prior to the event "I am the 2002 Commonwealth Games Individual Prone Champion".

Positive affirmations alone are insufficient—you still need to be performing well. Prior to every major event, the Australian Shooting Association held a training camp for the athletes, usually somewhere geographically closer to the host country than Australia. At the training camp, which was held in Germany on this occasion, I was shooting really well in training and in friendly competitions we held with our German hosts, who were all very strong shooters. There is nothing like good performances leading into a competition to give you some confidence in your skills and ability and add to your belief that you can win.

In the pairs event, held first at the Games, I finished with the second-highest score on the day so I went into the individual event four days later with good confidence. I went on to realise my dream and became the individual Commonwealth Champion for my event in 2002.

I am not suggesting that simply writing "I am the club pairs' champion" or "I am the national pairs' champion" is going to turn you into a champion bridge player or make you win, particularly if you are only an average player. You have to have the skills and ability to go with it. You also have to have a little bit of luck, but all things being equal, the competitor with a positive approach will have a much greater probability of succeeding than the competitor who approaches a match with a negative or neutral mindset. Positive affirmations are simply another way to facilitate a good mindset to help your performance.

Use good results to reinforce your performance

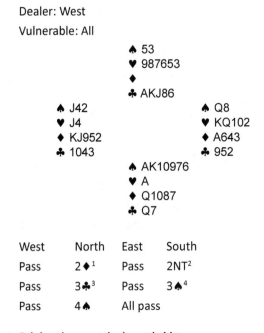

Dealer: West
Vulnerable: All

	♠ 53	
	♥ 987653	
	♦	
	♣ AKJ86	
♠ J42		♠ Q8
♥ J4		♥ KQ102
♦ KJ952		♦ A643
♣ 1043		♣ 952
	♠ AK10976	
	♥ A	
	♦ Q1087	
	♣ Q7	

West	North	East	South
Pass	2♦[1]	Pass	2NT[2]
Pass	3♣[3]	Pass	3♠[4]
Pass	4♠	All pass	

1 - Weak two in either major or 20 - 22 balanced.

2 - Forcing enquiry

3 - Good weak two in hearts

4 - Forcing to four spades or three no-trumps

On the deal above, the North hand is one where system agreements play a large part in the bidding decisions. Some players agree to open the North hand with a bid showing two suits, which might be attractive particularly when the heart suit is so poor. However, our agreement on hands like this is to give preference to the bid showing the six-card major over the two-suited options available in our system. I agree my heart suit here was truly awful and when my dummy appeared on the table, East raised an eyebrow at the 'good' weak two in hearts.

On West's lead of the two of spades, declarer took East's queen of spades with the ace and immediately ruffed a diamond. He returned to hand with a club back to the queen and drew one more round of trumps before playing a club across to dummy's ace of clubs. With the clubs breaking evenly, declarer could now discard two more diamonds on dummy's clubs before West could ruff in with his now high jack of spades. This loser on winner play produced eleven tricks for declarer with the loss of just one trump and one diamond.

This hand gave my partner and me a boost at this point in the competition. Making a contract where your system methods or style worked well for you provides a positive lift for your confidence. When your bidding has surprised the opponents it's even better, since it may make them take an action on another hand that is incorrect, as they dwell on a previous hand.

Saying to yourself at the end of such a hand "our system is working for us" or "my decision to open that hand was correct" will also reinforce a positive mindset and improve your confidence levels.

Avoid comments or thoughts that sub-consciously give you permission to fail

A top international bridge player I know, who had recently won one of our national competitions after a particularly close playoff where his team came from behind to win, mentioned to me that one of the opponents had stated during the final how tired he was. At the end of a long tournament everyone is tired—it doesn't matter how fit you are or whether your game is tennis, chess, bridge, golf or any other activity. In fact, if you aren't tired, you probably haven't been working hard enough during the matches. However, saying that you are tired, or feeling poorly because you have a headache or stomach ache or whatever, is just creating the excuse in your sub-conscious for when you fail. In a way, this is a method for dealing with the lack of belief that you can win. What's worse, however, is that saying something like this during the event gives your opponent(s) a mental boost and increases the likelihood that they will defeat you. This sort of comment costs you twice. Three times if you also think about the effect negative statements might have on your partner's performance during a match.

Next time you sit down to play a more highly ranked pair, or a pair against whom you think you have done poorly against in the past, adopt a positive mindset, keep your thoughts and comments positive and see how much you can put the opponents to the test. Maybe it will be your opponents who end up 'feeling tired' and creating excuses!

Chapter 4

Are you focussed?

"When walking, walk. When eating, eat."

- Zen Proverb

I have lost count of the number of times a player has told me they went off in a contract because the room was too noisy towards the end of the round or they passed without meaning to because they were thinking about something else. Dealing with distractions which occur during play is critical to success, particularly since distractions are pretty much an everyday occurrence in a bridge competition. Maintaining your focus and concentration in the face of distractions is a key element of every good player's skill set.

It is hard to say what causes good players to make fundamental errors, but clearly losing concentration or focus is a common occurrence. On this deal played in the final of Australia's biggest matchpoint pairs event where overtricks or undertricks are critical, our expert opponent made a simple error to give us an extra trick and 96% on the board.

Dealer: East

Vulnerable: E-W

		♠ K74	
		♥ J762	
		♦ QJ102	
		♣ K9	
♠ 53			♠ QJ1096
♥ Q10			♥ 9843
♦ A9643			♦ K5
♣ 8763			♣ A5
		♠ A82	
		♥ AK5	
		♦ 87	
		♣ QJ1042	

West	North	East	South
		Pass	1NT
Pass	2♣[1]	Pass	2♦[2]
Pass	3♣[3]	Pass	3NT[4]
All pass			

1 - Forces two diamonds

2 - Forced

3 - Puppet Stayman

4 - No four or five card major

East's king won the first trick after the diamond lead. At trick two she switched to the queen of spades, ducked all round. East continued with the jack of spades which was won by declarer's ace, with West signalling even count. Declarer played a low club to the king and ace. East now switched to the eight of hearts.

With eight sure tricks established, declarer won in hand with the ace of hearts and played a diamond towards dummy's queen which West ducked. On the run of the clubs, East pitched a heart. After the queen of hearts dropped doubleton declarer claimed the remainder for +430. West said afterwards "I didn't count declarer's points before playing to that trick and should have risen with the ace to save the overtrick." Indeed!

What happened here? West lost focus or his concentration became distracted by something other than what the defence needed. Perhaps it was something external or perhaps West was thinking about a previous hand or something that had happened earlier. He went into 'autopilot mode' and suddenly an innocuous hand had turned into a disaster. This chapter discusses how we can avoid this happening in bridge, and indeed in other areas of our lives.

Prepare for how to deal with distractions before the event

My second major international shooting competition was the 1994 Commonwealth Games. The public in Australia have a passionate interest in the Commonwealth Games. It's a big deal with extensive TV coverage, thousands of competitors in multiple events and a lot of press and publicity, both in the lead-up and at the actual event.

When I walked into the shooting range on the practice day, I found that right behind my allocated shooting position was a TV camera. Some sportspeople experience TV cameras all the time, but in shooting this was definitely a new experience for me. It would be fair to say that I had never competed anywhere previously where there had been TV cameras. Nevertheless, my pre-event preparation had included rehearsing specifically for this scenario, thanks to some wonderful tapes I had listened to from the Olympian Lanny Bassham, which described this exact scenario happening to him. In these tapes he spoke about how the presence of the camera caused him to become so nervous that he started poorly in the match. The poor start cost him so many points that it was impossible to score highly enough in the remainder of the match to enable him to win the gold medal.

On match day, I found that while I was in the preparation stage of the match it was definitely unnerving to have the idea of that little red light watching me as I progressed through the competition. However, once I started my match, I focussed on what I had practiced—firing each shot. I can honestly say that once I started my match, I didn't give the camera another thought. I was able to maintain my focus during the whole match rather than being distracted by the idea of being on TV. In that match, my partner and I went on to win the gold medal for Australia in what was the first medal decided at those games.

Consider how detrimental to my performance it might have been if I hadn't prepared properly by practicing for this scenario occurring and my thoughts had strayed to think about how many people were watching and what they might be thinking as I progressed through my match?

While TV cameras are also a rarity in the bridge world, spectators (known in the bridge world as kibitzers) are more common. Early on in my bridge playing days I was playing at a national event where there was a kibitzer who asked to sit at the table. I had no idea about kibitzers at the time and I found it more than a little distracting. I just wasn't prepared for it at the time.

Imagine having the distraction of a kibitzer at your table when presented with this hand on the first board of the round:

Dealer: West
Vulnerable: Both

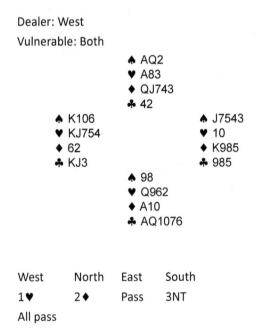

West	North	East	South
1♥	2♦	Pass	3NT
All pass			

West led the spade six, which was ducked to East's jack. East returned the heart ten ducked all round, followed by the eight of clubs to declarer's ten and won by West's jack. West continued with the jack of hearts which was run to declarer's queen. The contract should have been easily made from this point with declarer holding control of all suits had declarer simply played the ace and then ten of diamonds and letting it run. However, clearly distracted by the kibitzer instead of focussing on the play, declarer counted dummy's diamonds as six instead of five. So instead of running the ten of diamonds he overtook and then claimed, stating he would run the diamonds and give up a heart at the end. Naturally the opponents disputed that claim and the contract was ruled one off.

Going off in a cold contract because you lost concentration is a poor way to start a round. Kibitzers are just one kind of distraction that can occur. There are all kinds of other distractions such as: noisy playing areas; other players talking about hands; bad play; bad defence; director calls; comments by partner; being on BBO, and so on.

Being prepared for whatever the competition throws up at you is part of achieving success. In shooting, like in bridge, matches and events are often won by a fraction of a point—sometimes even by countback when the scores are tied. Think about how many tournaments in which you have played where the winning margin has been very small—one or two victory points or matchpoints or even less. How many times might you have won instead of lost an event if one or two hands had gone slightly differently? In a game like bridge where the edges and margins are very small, it is all the things you do to prepare that allow you to gain those few extra points that are the difference between winning and losing. Every little bit adds up.

Do you allow thoughts of previous hands to occupy your mind?

I am sure we have all observed bridge players who allow a distraction or incident in the playing room to interfere with their play. Many players will dwell on an incident from an earlier deal in their round, such as a director ruling, the play of a hand, a bidding sequence or poor defence instead of focussing on the current hand. In fact, some players become so upset by these distractions that they misplay or misbid subsequent hands because they don't have a means of focussing on the task at hand and blotting out the other stuff.

It is not uncommon to see players deep in thought before they make their bid. Quite often they are not thinking about what to bid now—they are processing the previous deal to the detriment of the current task. Being able to re-focus on the task at hand is a key mental tool that will help you enhance your overall performance. Having a plan for what you will do when distractions occur is an integral part of this plan.

Consider the following deal which was an unusual miss by a generally strong player towards the end of a match when in contention for a placing:

Dealer: West
Vulnerable: All

```
                    ♠ 4
                    ♥ AQJ9875
                    ♦ Q4
                    ♣ 987
        ♠ J976                      ♠ AQ83
        ♥ K64                       ♥ 2
        ♦ 93                        ♦ 10652
        ♣ Q642                      ♣ KJ105
                    ♠ K1052
                    ♥ 103
                    ♦ AKJ87
                    ♣ A3
```

West	North	East	South
Pass	Pass[1]	Pass	1NT
Pass	2♦[2]	Pass	2♥
Pass	4♥	All pass	

1 - Unusual to pass in second seat instead of pre-empting 3♥
2 - Transfer to hearts

South ended up declarer in four hearts after a transfer sequence following a strong no-trump opening. On the lie of the cards, twelve tricks are possible provided the heart finesse is taken (even thirteen on a non-spade lead) with declarer simply finessing twice in trumps before throwing dummy's clubs on the winning diamonds. Even without the finesse, it is hard to imagine a line which would fail, yet our normally reliable player did just that and failed to make the vulnerable game.

On the lead of the nine of diamonds, declarer won in dummy and decided to play for hearts to be 2-2. He played ace of hearts and a low heart to his ten won by West's king, with East signalling for a club switch with the five of clubs. West duly exited a low club won by declarer's ace, leaving this position:

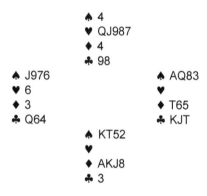

Unable to return to dummy to draw the outstanding trump before taking advantage of the high diamonds, declarer must now lose two clubs and a spade, in addition to the trump king, for one off.

This and the previous deal illustrate how an unfocussed or distracted player might go down in a contract they would normally make. The reasons why a strong player makes an uncharacteristic error in play are not always obvious—perhaps being the last round and being in contention made a difference? Or perhaps it was the fact that the opponents had already made a slam and a marginal three no-trumps that caused a loss of concentration here? Or maybe he was just distracted by the failure of his partner to open the hand three hearts in the first place? Clearly something interfered with the player's normally reliable play and caused the poor performance on this board.

While some players are fortunate and can maintain their focus during an earthquake, many are not so lucky. Let's explore how to deal with distractions in more detail by firstly classing these distractions as two types—external and internal.

Type 1 Distractions: External

Type 1 distractions are those which occur 'outside your head'. They are external to you and are predictable events which often happen at tournaments. These incidents occur in the playing area near enough to you for you to see or hear them and to attract (or distract) your attention. They might not happen at every tournament, but there is a reasonable frequency of occurrence. They include things like:

- » director calls to tables nearby;
- » loud noises;
- » things being dropped;
- » players spilling drinks on the table;
- » players leaving the table during play (yours or a nearby table);
- » players chattering at your table or another table;
- » kibitzers;
- » phones ringing;
- » someone falling ill and requiring medical attention;
- » and so on...

Have you ever been playing at a tournament and seen players become distracted by an incident at a neighbouring table? Think about how many times you've then seen them turn their attention back to the hand they are about to play and pass without having seen their partner's bid! Oops! They now call the director to the table saying they passed by accident and find out their bid has to stand. They become frazzled and annoyed by their mistake and it may take a couple of hands for them to re-focus by which time the match is already lost. One distraction causing an error is something many players will have experienced or observed at some time in their lives.

These types of external distractions are those which you can and should plan for and work out what you are going to do when they occur. I have listed above many of the most common types of these distractions and recommend that you make a plan for what you are going to do to manage them if and when they occur. There is no right answer here and it is important you decide what will work for you, but here are some suggestions.

To give an example of how this works, let's imagine the players at the next table spill a drink all over the cards and start creating a ruckus, which is distracting for your table. If you are a player who is oblivious to these distractions you might be able to carry on, but your opponents might ask you to wait. This might be annoying or distracting to you, particularly if you are in the middle of playing a hand. Think about how you are going to overcome your annoyance and maintain your concentration. Alternatively, if you are a player that is easily distracted, then you may wish to plan that you will stop play until the activity at the next table calms down, rather than trying to play while distracted with your concentration divided and then going off in a game you should make because you cannot concentrate with all the peripheral noise.

If your plan is to stop and wait, then you might also plan how you will manage this with the opponents. For example, rehearse saying something to the other players at your table like "I'm sorry, but I just can't concentrate with all this going on at the next table. Would you mind if we just wait a moment until things calm down?". Letting the opponents know that you are going to have a pause in play helps manage the situation and avoid a confrontation. Think about how you will respond if the opponents suggest you continue to play, and so on.

You might also plan for how you will get yourself 'back into the hand' after a disturbance. Taking a quick recap of the last trick, the number of tricks each side has, the contract, the bidding, the opening lead... these can all be ways to re-enter a focussed state.

The list above is not exhaustive and you may have other incidents that have occurred in the past that you found distracting. Think about those incidents and what you might do differently next time to avoid the same thing happening. The important thing is to rehearse in your mind what you will do in the event that any of them occur. Get your partner onside with your strategy, too. The idea here is to be prepared so that if and when something does happen you know how to deal with it and it doesn't throw you and your partner off your game.

Type 2 Distractions: Internal

Type 2 distractions are internal to you - i.e. 'inside your head' and which preoccupy your thoughts. These include those situations where:

- » you have made an error or perceive you have made an error;

- » your partner has made an error, e.g. a revoke, dropped a card, underbid, etc., and this error is occupying your thoughts;

- » the opponents have made a contract you 'think' you should have defeated;

- » the opponents have bid a contract which you 'think' might be a match winner;

- » you are physically tired or unwell;

» you have something on your mind from work or an event that happened earlier in the day;

» and so on....

Let's consider one of the most common distractions which players will face. This occurs when you have just had a board where you failed to make a makeable contract. Keen observers of players at bridge will have noted when a player's mind has clearly gone elsewhere part way through the match. Letting go of that board and regaining focus for the next one is critical to success at the bridge table.

Here is a hand from a teams competition where I went off in a three no-trump contract that I thought I should have made. It was one of those hands with too many options and it felt like any one of several lines should have succeeded.

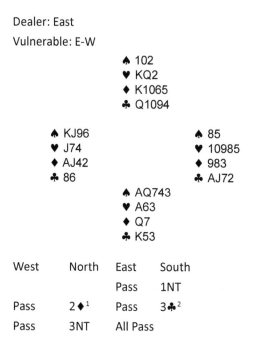

Dealer: East
Vulnerable: E-W

	♠ 102	
	♥ KQ2	
	♦ K1065	
	♣ Q1094	

♠ KJ96		♠ 85
♥ J74		♥ 10985
♦ AJ42		♦ 983
♣ 86		♣ AJ72

	♠ AQ743	
	♥ A63	
	♦ Q7	
	♣ K53	

West	North	East	South
		Pass	1NT
Pass	2♦[1]	Pass	3♣[2]
Pass	3NT	All Pass	

1 - Any Game Force

2 - Five spades and unknown 332 shape in other suits.

(hand repeated below)

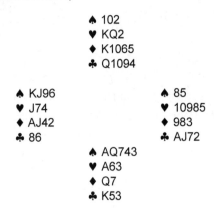

```
                    ♠ 102
                    ♥ KQ2
                    ♦ K1065
                    ♣ Q1094
     ♠ KJ96                        ♠ 85
     ♥ J74                         ♥ 10985
     ♦ AJ42                        ♦ 983
     ♣ 86                          ♣ AJ72
                    ♠ AQ743
                    ♥ A63
                    ♦ Q7
                    ♣ K53
```

West got off to an excellent lead with the eight of clubs. Looking at dummy I could see three hearts, one diamond, one club and one spade trick, with several possible lines to create the extra tricks.

One chance was that spades could break 3-3. If the spade finesse worked that would also help create the extra tricks. Unfortunately, after dummy's nine of clubs was covered by the jack and king, I chose the wrong line when I elected to try to establish the spades by crossing to dummy's king of hearts and finessing the queen of spades (playing a low spade towards the ten would have been superior). West continued with the six of clubs, covered by dummy's ten and won by East's ace.

East exited safely for the defence with a heart won by dummy's queen. I continued with the ten of spades to the ace and another spade. I hoped spades would break, but this was not to be. When West showed up with the diamond ace as well, the defence had five tricks.

While not necessarily a simple contract to make, it was nevertheless one that would have been easy to dwell on after the board was finished making it difficult to focus on the next board. There were so many different ways that things could have gone better for me, but dwelling on it might be distracting for a long time and cause errors on subsequent boards.

In these circumstances, I like to take a drink and a deep breath and tell myself to focus as I pick up my cards for the next board to make sure I don't compound the error or perceived error just made. As it happens the next board where I became declarer in three spades required some careful play to make.

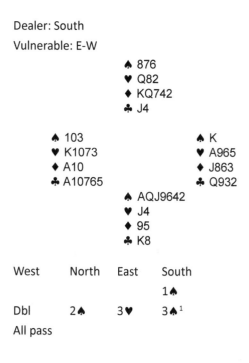

Dealer: South
Vulnerable: E-W

```
                    ♠ 876
                    ♥ Q82
                    ♦ KQ742
                    ♣ J4
      ♠ 103                        ♠ K
      ♥ K1073                      ♥ A965
      ♦ A10                        ♦ J863
      ♣ A10765                     ♣ Q932
                    ♠ AQJ9642
                    ♥ J4
                    ♦ 95
                    ♣ K8
```

West	North	East	South
			1♠
Dbl	2♠	3♥	3♠[1]
All pass			

1 - Competitive – not invitational

When dummy came down after the lead of the ace of diamonds by West, eight tricks were obvious and I could see several options for the ninth trick. It looked like the club ace was going to be sitting badly after West's double, so on the ten of diamonds continuation, I won with dummy's king and continued with the queen of diamonds pitching a losing heart while West ruffed and kindly exited a spade, locating the king for me.

West could have done better by switching to a heart after which East could have put a club through, thus making life far more difficult for me. After the spade exit, I was able to use dummy's spades to set up a long diamond trick for a second heart pitch and the contract. Now my partner and I felt like we were 'even' and the opponents had to deal with the possible distraction of wondering how the defence might have gone differently.

These two boards are examples of common occurrences at the bridge table. We all have a bad board now and then or a contract we think or know we should have made or defeated. However being able to put that result aside to focus on the next board is critical to success. Compounding an error by making another one is a recipe for disaster. Being able to re-focus after a bad or perceived bad board is a skill worth acquiring.

Even with all the knowledge of preparation and focus, there are still times where good players will make a simple error which causes a bad board. In these circumstances, re-focussing your attention is a key to success. Here's what happened to me in an evening competition when I walked out of a meeting which ran overtime and started play at the table a few minutes later. On this occasion the first board off the pile saw my partner and me (East-West) on defence against three no-trumps:

Dealer: South
Vulnerable: N-S

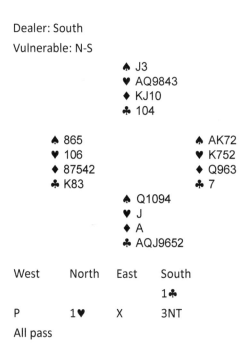

	♠ J3		
	♥ AQ9843		
	♦ KJ10		
	♣ 104		

```
              ♠ J3
              ♥ AQ9843
              ♦ KJ10
              ♣ 104
♠ 865                      ♠ AK72
♥ 106                      ♥ K752
♦ 87542                    ♦ Q963
♣ K83                      ♣ 7
              ♠ Q1094
              ♥ J
              ♦ A
              ♣ AQJ9652
```

West	North	East	South
			1♣
P	1♥	X	3NT
All pass			

My partner (West) led the seven of diamonds (second highest from a bad suit). The play proceeded ten, queen, ace. South continued with the two of clubs which West ducked to North's ten. Realising the clubs might be dead, declarer continued with the three of spades from dummy taken by East's ace who came back with the three of diamonds taken by dummy's jack.

As East, I should have thought a bit more at this point and counted out the diamond suit, paying particular attention to the pips before quitting the trick so that I could take advantage of the situation which emerged. Sadly, my mind wasn't really at the table yet and I failed to do this most basic task. When declarer played the jack of spades from dummy, I won with the king and I should now have unblocked the diamond suit by playing the nine. Instead I returned the six of diamonds which left this end position after declarer won with dummy's king:

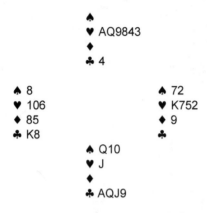

```
                    ♠
                    ♥ AQ9843
                    ♦
                    ♣ 4
    ♠ 8                          ♠ 72
    ♥ 106                        ♥ K752
    ♦ 85                         ♦ 9
    ♣ K8                         ♣
                    ♠ Q10
                    ♥ J
                    ♦
                    ♣ AQJ9
```

When declarer played the four of clubs the club situation was confirmed and declarer won the ace in hand. He now cashed his two spade winners and played the jack of hearts, overtaken with dummy's queen and won by East's king. Now the consequences of my failure to unblock the diamonds were clear and I had no alternative other than to cash my winning diamond and give declarer the last two tricks in hearts.

This was not a particularly tricky defence. Any experienced player should have had no difficulty counting the diamond suit and unblocking. However, on this hand, I wasn't 'at the table' yet and I wasn't focussed 100% on the play. Consequently I made a simple error. Needless to say, my partner wasn't happy and a reminder to pay attention helped get me re-focussed for the next deal (and the rest of the session which went much better with my attention focussed at the table). It is possible to win after a bad start, but it is much easier if you don't have to.[1]

It can be hard for some players to allow their mind to let go of these internal distractions and focus properly, but it is important to be able to do this to play at your optimal level. Developing ways to deal with these distractions will help ensure you remain focussed.

---

1   Note that on this hand declarer can always make three no-trumps by leading the jack of hearts at trick two, overtaking with the queen and continuing with the ace of hearts. When the ten drops on the second round, declarer should continue with the hearts until East wins with the king of hearts. Given the position of the king of clubs, the ten becomes an entry, and the best the defence can do is take one heart, one club and two spades.

How to deal with internal distractions

There are many different methods for dealing with internal distractions. Some players deal with internal distractions by making a note to themselves about the issue they think happened, so that they can consider it later. Making a note can have the effect of 'giving yourself permission' to let the incident go and act as a reminder to discuss it later. Some players hate making notes on their scoresheet because they think it might give the opponents a clue that something has gone wrong.

If notes don't work for you and you cannot let an incident go or you need to do something to change the momentum, consider excusing yourself from the table for a bathroom break, to get a drink or some other time-out so that you have a short pause to get over the incident. Each match usually has more than enough time in each round to do this, especially at major events. Unless you are exceptionally slow players there is always time to have a little break to get over a stuff-up or to give yourself time to let some issue go. Naturally you cannot leave the table every time you have a bad board (or a board that you think was bad), but you can have different tactics that you employ from time to time to regroup after a distraction.

Re-focussing your distracted partner

Similarly, finding ways to help your partner overcome their own internal or external distractions is also important. Here's an example of how this worked in practice for me.

Several years ago, playing an event with my partner of the time, we kicked off the tournament in the first round with a few disastrous boards: things like going off in a cold game, passing out of turn, and so on. Having dropped around thirty IMPs after the third disaster in five boards, I apologised to the opponents for requiring a bathroom break so soon after we started and left the table. I had planned for this kind of occurrence and felt that I needed to do something to break the negative momentum and give my partner and me time to regroup. Giving partner a moment to settle and re-focus worked on that occasion and we ended up playing well enough on the remaining boards to tie the match with our opponents despite the dreadful start.

Another player told me that something that worked for him and a partner of his who had to understand what had happened and process it after a disaster was to very briefly clarify whatever had gone wrong: e.g. "sorry, I thought my last diamond was a winner. Let's move on."

Alternatively, when you see your partner's concentration has wandered, a word or phrase at the table to re-focus their attention on the task at hand will often help. Something like "partner, are you with us?" or "next board, partner—concentrate", will often be enough to get partner's mind back on track.

Get your partner onside with your strategy

Since bridge is very much a partnership game, helping each other manage distractions is equally important. For example, if you tend to dwell on the hand that you have just played and stuffed up, your partner can help you re-focus by using a cue-word that draws your attention to your mind wandering. Similarly, if you have just had what you think is a disastrous board, one of you could excuse yourself for a moment to grab a quick drink or bathroom break. Naturally leaving the table multiple times in a match isn't an option, but used judiciously this can be a useful tactic to ensure you or your partner have time to recover from a disaster and re-focus. It is also important for you to discuss with each other how and when you will employ these tactics. It isn't very helpful if your partner thinks you have left the table in a huff because partner just went off in a contract that should have been made.

Pre-match preparation

Closely aligned with dealing with distractions during the event is preparing yourself so that you are 'ready to play' when you arrive at the event and that you have considered what might occur to prevent you playing at your best at an event.

When I was competing at shooting I had prepared a list identifying what could go wrong or happen during the whole tournament. I mentally rehearsed what I was going to do if such and such happened in competition for each item on my list. This type of preparation is just as important as practicing your system with your partner.

When considering your pre-match preparation in bridge, there are five key questions to ask yourself:

> » What can go wrong before I leave home?
>
> » What can go wrong at the event?
>
> » What can go wrong during play?
>
> » How will I react?
>
> » What can I do to limit the potential damage?

Here's an example of how this might work if you are properly prepared for something that might happen in an event such as on this deal, where our explanation of the bidding was challenged.

Dealer: North
Vulnerable: All

```
                        ♠ Q94
                        ♥ J10532
                        ♦ 102
                        ♣ A92
        ♠ K832                          ♠ J1076
        ♥ 64                            ♥ AKQ87
        ♦ J873                          ♦ KQ
        ♣ J108                          ♣ Q3
                        ♠ A5
                        ♥ 9
                        ♦ A9654
                        ♣ K7654
```

West	North	East	South
	Pass	1NT	2♥¹
Pass	2♠²	Pass	3♣
All pass			

1 - Single Suiter in spades or both minors

2 - Pass or correct

Before leading, West asked about the alert on the two-heart bid by South and was told it now showed both minors and was normally 5-5, but if South had a stronger hand it could be 5-4 either way.

The defence led two rounds of hearts, ruffed by declarer. After a club to the ace, dummy's jack of hearts was covered by East's queen, ruffed by declarer and overruffed by West, who continued with a low diamond around to declarer's ace. Declarer now cashed the king of clubs, drawing the remaining trumps before playing a diamond towards dummy's ten on which East played his now singleton king. Having lost three tricks to this point, declarer only lost a spade trick and three clubs rolled home. The contract can be defeated on a different lead, but on this defence three clubs made nine tricks.

At the conclusion of play West challenged the explanation I had provided on the hand. My partner calmly laid out his hand and showed his shape to be exactly as I had described. This sort of situation where someone makes it clear they feel hard done by can be confrontational and distracting. It is essential to have a strategy for dealing with it. At the time it was unclear to me exactly why West had a problem, but calmly defusing the situation was the best solution in this situation. In retrospect West may simply have been venting frustration after an unsatisfying defence.

Considering how you will deal with situations like this should they arise is a fundamental part of pre-match preparation.

Here's another example of how this pre-match preparation can work for you:

What can go wrong during play?

You have revoked and your revoke allowed the opponents to make a contract you could have defeated. Your partner looks upset with you since you have done this before when you get a bit tired later in the day. You know that part of the reason partner is upset is because when this has happened in the past, you have also tended to make another simple mistake on the next board.

How will I react?

Apologise to partner for your error and take a moment to re-focus and to give partner time to settle down. Have a drink of water, take a deep breath, and say to yourself a focussing word like 'concentrate'.

What can I do to limit the potential damage?

Before starting the next board, say to yourself, "that board is gone, focus on the next board" or use a cue-word as described in the next section. Slow down and think carefully during play on the next board before playing each card or making a bid so that you don't make another silly mistake.

Developing strategies to manage the answers to these questions for all the common situations which arise will help you to play at your optimal level and ensure you don't give away points unnecessarily. Working on proper match preparation is a critical part of increasing your chances of success in competition bridge.

Visualising your performance

Any of us who have watched top level sport on television will have observed athletes in various sports standing and waiting before taking their attempt at a jump or shot or before starting their race. Golfers will stand and visualise in their mind where they want to hit the ball before they do it. High jumpers will stand and look at the bar and picture themselves executing a successful jump before they take their attempt. Basketballers picture themselves throwing the ball through the hoop before they take a free throw. Whenever it is possible, athletes in all types of sport use mental rehearsal before executing their performance. What they are doing is visualising their performance or shot or jump before doing it.

Exactly the same idea can be used when you are playing bridge. A top player once told me that he visualises the contract level he thinks might be possible based on his hand before he makes his first bid. How effectively this works is difficult to say, but I have observed that his decisions on bidding are right more often than not. Maybe this is a tactic worth consideration.

Consider picking up the following hand as West:

♠ Q10 ♥ AKQ965 ♦ A1082 ♣ A

What contract do you think might be possible? What about if partner deals and passes? What about if partner is not a passed hand? What about if the opponents open the bidding? And so on?

When I was dealt the above hand, my initial thought was, "this looks like a hand where I want to be in game". Here's what happened at the table:

Dealer: North

Vulnerable: N-S

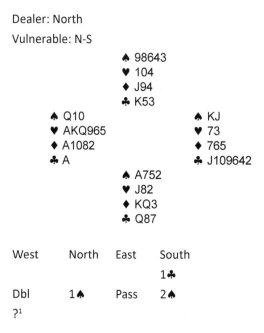

```
                        ♠ 98643
                        ♥ 104
                        ♦ J94
                        ♣ K53
        ♠ Q10                           ♠ KJ
        ♥ AKQ965                        ♥ 73
        ♦ A1082                         ♦ 765
        ♣ A                             ♣ J109642
                        ♠ A752
                        ♥ J82
                        ♦ KQ3
                        ♣ Q87
```

West	North	East	South
			1♣
Dbl	1♠	Pass	2♠
?[1]			

1 - what would you bid here?

In practice, I didn't think through my bidding options for long enough after the bidding started and at the decision point I chose to bid three hearts (highly encouraging, but not 100% forcing), which was where I ended up playing. On reflection, while three hearts seems like a perfectly normal bid to make on this hand three spades asking partner to bid three no-trumps with a stopper might be considered by some to be a logical alternative to three hearts. With what looks like eight tricks in my hand assuming a reasonable heart distribution, plus the queen of spades, three no-trumps looks like a good chance if partner can win a spade trick.

Ten tricks in hearts can also be made since diamonds split 3-3, but my choice of bids left us languishing in a part-score. Had I properly thought more about the likely continuations which bidding three hearts might bring, I may have chosen a different bid. Mentally playing through the different options and visualising what will happen as a result of an action is an important skill.

Using cue-words to focus and re-focus

In shooting, I would mentally rehearse every shot I made both in practice and in competition before firing the shot. Over time it became automatic to rehearse before each shot and it only took a few seconds each time. My mental rehearsal started after I loaded the rifle. I would run through in my mind the perfect shot sequence that I wanted to perform, then execute it (no pun intended!). At the end of running the mental rehearsal I would think the word 'ten' (my shooting cue-word) and picture the sight centred on the target. This 'cue word' was the instruction to my mind to focus. After running my mental rehearsal and saying the cue word, I was at the point of initiation and 'ready to go', after which my mind was now focussed on firing the shot and not on anything else, including any distractions that might have been present at the venue.

I will cover mental rehearsal in detail in Chapter 6 (refer page 102), but it is appropriate to mention one technique here because it is so relevant to creating and maintaining focus. Using this type of mental program at the bridge table may also assist players to concentrate and ensure focus is maintained during a hand by setting the mind up for performance. Moreover, if we lose concentration, use of the cue-word can be used to regain focus. If athletes can use cue-words to focus, then it seems logical that bridge players can also do it. Here is how this type of technique can work in bridge. There are two parts to every hand.

- » Part one is the bidding;
- » Part two is the play, whether as declarer or defender.

Before commencing part one, you could use a cue word to get your mind on the job at the point of initiation. I suggest in bridge this is the point just before you take the cards out of the board (or after dealing the hand).

The cue word could be anything that works for you, but it should be an action word. Choose something like attention, focus, count or some other relevant word to get your mind to wake up to the fact you are about to initiate the bidding sequence. One of my friends joked to me about using 'silver bullet' as my word. Later in the match after he had made this remark, he used that as a cue-word to make me re-focus when I had made a critical error in defence.

The cue word is a signal to your mind to pay attention and stop worrying about distractions around the room, the last hand, etc. This will also help you relax if you are little bit nervous. Our mind likes routine and there is certainly a routine to this part of the hand. For example, a basic routine that happens at the start of the hand which you could run mentally is something like:

- » Focus (the cue word);

- » Check I am picking up my seat's cards (the board orientation);

- » Count my cards;

- » Check my hand is sorted properly with all cards of the same suit together;

- » Check who is dealer;

- » Check the vulnerability;

- » Count my points;

- » Consider my first bid and likely continuations;

- » Wait for my turn to bid.

Note that this is not an exhaustive list of all your considerations when the bidding is about to start, but it is a basic routine surrounding what normally happens at the start of a board. It will help to get your mind on track and assist your concentration. It also only takes a few seconds to run this through your mind mentally. It will get you focussed on the current hand and help forget the previous board, distractions in the room and so on. Over time as you become familiar with this, the list could become a series of words which act like prompts such as: focus; orientation; count; sort; dealer; vulnerability; points; opening; wait.

Having a routine will also help you overcome nervousness and block out distractions. Just like a high jumper rehearses the jump they are about to make, and a shooter rehearses the next shot, having a routine at the card table will help you to focus and maintain concentration.

When the auction is finished, there is often a short break in concentration while some housekeeping happens, like entering the contract, notes on scoresheets and so on. Before commencing part 2, the play of the hand, you want to re-focus. Use the same word to help get your mind back on track for this part of the game. I also suggest avoiding a word like 'lead' — it might make you lead out of turn!

The cue word is the signal to your mind to focus, and it can be used at any time during the match. To an experienced player the above mental program might seem a bit simplistic, but the aim is to reach a point where re-focussing can be done quite quickly by simply saying your cue word.

Occasionally however, even top players may become so focussed on a particular aspect of play that they forget the basics. This deal was from the 2018 Platinum Pairs in Philadelphia:

Dealer: North
Vulnerable: E-W

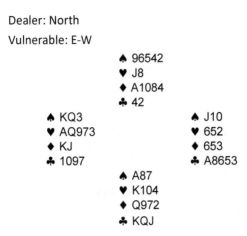

♠ 96542
♥ J8
♦ A1084
♣ 42

♠ KQ3
♥ AQ973
♦ KJ
♣ 1097

♠ J10
♥ 652
♦ 653
♣ A8653

♠ A87
♥ K104
♦ Q972
♣ KQJ

South opened 1NT after two passes and North transferred to two spades which became the final contract.

West led the ten of clubs to East's ace. East returned a heart. West cashed two hearts and then played a third round. Dummy pitched a diamond as declarer won in hand.

Declarer played a low spade, which was ducked around to East's ten. East returned a club. Declarer won and cashed the ace of spades, the remaining club honour and then played a low spade, 'endplaying' West who was down to all red cards. Declarer, however, had no-trumps left, a fact lost on West.

The conversation at the table then went something like this:

As the club was cashed and spade exited to West, he said — "Yep, nice play. Nice play."

Then West, believing he really was endplayed, led the jack of diamonds!

One second later: "Oh shit! Sorry! Sorry. Sorry."

Declarer shrugs and says, "Well, I guess I'll play low…"

West, after declarer won the queen of diamonds: "He had no more trumps left… I could've played a heart. I was so fixated on the endplay". The lapse allowed two spades to make.

Everyone at the table were international players. Lack of focus is a universal affliction.

Take 'mental breaks'

Cue words are not enough when we are getting tired or the match is long. It is a well-known fact that the mind has a limited attention span before it needs a 'mental break'. Stress and other factors may also influence the amount of time the mind can effectively concentrate without a break. Given that bridge matches or segments can last for over two hours, planning mental breaks and using cue words to re-focus your attention can ensure you maintain an appropriate level of focus during your whole competition and avoid those costly lapses in concentration that might occur without a mental management plan.

Like many, I have found that most of my errors in bridge come from playing or bidding too fast. That happened on this next deal where my bid of five diamonds was made without enough thought.

This is an example where a loss of concentration at the end of the day in the final round of a tournament resulted in a bid which led to a poor outcome for us. Had I taken more time to consider the bidding, I might have chosen to pass, which would have been a better action.

Here's what happened:

Dealer: South
Vulnerable: E-W

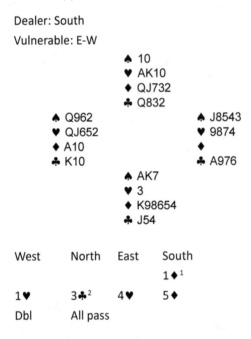

♠ 10
♥ AK10
♦ QJ732
♣ Q832

♠ Q962
♥ QJ652
♦ A10
♣ K10

♠ J8543
♥ 9874
♦
♣ A976

♠ AK7
♥ 3
♦ K98654
♣ J54

West	North	East	South
			1♦¹
1♥	3♣²	4♥	5♦
Dbl	All pass		

1 - five or more diamonds
2 - 10+HCP diamond raise

At the time, I overrated my singleton heart and assumed our values would be working for us instead of considering that partner might have heart values. However, it really wasn't my decision. Slowing down and thinking more carefully might have led to the correct decision. Pass would have conveyed the same meaning after my opening bid—happy to go on and it's up to you to decide, partner—while double would have clearly been penalty.

Bidding five diamonds on this hand meant our final result in the tournament was fourth instead of second. Certainly, there were other hands in the tournament that could also have had different outcomes, but this hand was an error and what you do in the last round tends to stick with you. As the match is drawing to a close use of your cue word before each board is one way to help prevent lapses like this one and to remind yourself to pay attention.

Obviously when you are dummy you should try to allow your mind to rest a little bit. You can let yourself be mostly 'switched off', only keeping track of play, whose lead it is, tricks won or lost and making sure there isn't a revoke or some other infraction that needs highlighting at the end of the deal. You are concentrating, but not with the same intensity as when you are playing the hand as declarer or defender.

In between hands is also an opportunity to 'switch off' a little bit. Have a drink, take a breath, have a stretch, before taking the cards out and using your cue-word to re-focus on the next board. In a long match, a bathroom or drink break at around the mid-point might be useful to enable a little mental break for both you and your partner as long as you are ahead of time in the match, particularly if you have just had a disaster on a board.

Finally, ensuring you maintain adequate energy levels with some snacks will also help—see page 166 on nutrition.

A final thought on distractions

The hardest type of 'distractions' to manage are those of a personal nature, such as a sick child or spouse, a health issue and other personal issues of this nature. No matter how well you prepare, these types of unexpected issues are often so significant that playing your best bridge, or even continuing to play, is extremely difficult. In these circumstances, if you choose to continue to play you might remind yourself why you have chosen to do so. There have been many cases reported in the media of top-level athletes who have done well in an event because they used personal circumstances such as a sick relation to motivate them to succeed.

You might also tell your partner and team-mates about the issue and make sure they understand that you might be distracted at times so that they can help you to re-focus at those times.

Remember, each player is different. What works for one might not work for another. Just as you test conventions to see if you like using them, testing what works best for you to manage your concentration levels is part of your overall improvement process. It is up to you to evaluate individually and as a partnership what is best for your circumstances.

Chapter 5

Comfort Zones

"I don't like to be out of my comfort zone which is about a half inch wide"

- Larry David, comedian; co-creator of Seinfeld

Everyone has a 'comfort zone' for pretty much everything they do, whether it is driving a car, typing a document, delivering a speech at work, playing sport or competing at bridge. A comfort zone is part of your self-confidence and belief in your own ability and skills. It is the degree of certainty you possess about your ability to be successful in the activity.

In sporting terms, a comfort zone is created over time from one's experiences, skill level and prior performances.

While top level players thrive on bidding and making big hands, less experienced players struggle when presented with an opportunity to bid a grand slam since doing so is outside their comfort zone. The following hand was bid seventeen times in a competition with only one pair managing to reach the laydown grand and over 50% failing to reach even the small slam. At our table, our interference left the opponents in four hearts, yet even with interference it should have been possible for North to push on to at least a small slam.

Dealer: North
Vulnerable: None

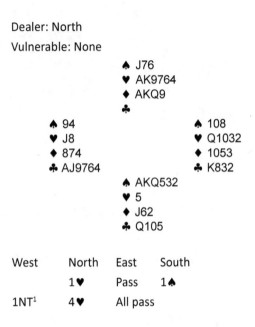

	♠ J76		
	♥ AK9764		
	♦ AKQ9		
	♣		

♠ 94		♠ 108	
♥ J8		♥ Q1032	
♦ 874		♦ 1053	
♣ AJ9764		♣ K832	

	♠ AKQ532		
	♥ 5		
	♦ J62		
	♣ Q105		

West	North	East	South
	1♥	Pass	1♠
1NT[1]	4♥	All pass	

1 - 'Comic' — weak single suited hand or 15 – 18 balanced

The comic one no-trump overcall worked exceptionally well here, but North could have done much better with either a double or a three-diamond bid showing a strong hand. Either of these options would have allowed South to rebid the spade suit. It is unlikely the bidding at other tables matched ours, although perhaps some West players tried a pre-emptive three club bid. Even so, North would have had an opportunity to show the powerful hand with either a double or another forcing bid. Were our opponents outside their comfort zone or simply outside their skill level? Either way it is hard to credit that more than 50% failed to reach even the small slam. Most likely it was due to being in an infrequent scenario where they didn't have the methods or experience to bid the grand slam. It could be said that they were outside their comfort zone. Perhaps our bidding pushed them outside their comfort zone. They simply were not equipped to find out the information they needed to reach a slam after the interference.

How do we obtain our comfort zone?

When we start any new activity, we don't really have a comfort zone for it. We are improving all the time. As our skill level grows and we are able to perform the activity at an increasing level of competence, our comfort zone grows as well. The rate of improvement will vary from person to person. Those with natural aptitude for an activity will improve more quickly than others. Over time we reach a point where improvement slows and it requires significant work to achieve increases in performance outcomes. This is where the hard work really begins.

If we consider a golfer who always scores between 75 and 80 shots for a round of golf, we would say that scoring range is their comfort zone. They are happy scoring in that range and they will generally be relaxed on the golf course as long as they are on target to achieve that score. If they have a poor start, they will often finish strongly allowing them to finish with a score that is within their comfort zone. Their self-talk (the little voice inside your head) will say something like, "it's not like me to score 45 on the opening 9 holes", and the golfer might become angry or embarrassed about performing poorly.

While anger is an emotion which can overcome fear, it may also cause reckless behaviour. The angry player will usually find this leads to one of two outcomes—either the golfer will use the anger about their poor performance to focus properly and pull their score back in the latter half of the round to finish with 80 or 81, which is right on the upper edge of their comfort zone. Or they will allow their anger (or rage) to control their actions and throw caution to the wind usually ending up with an even worse result.

Similarly, if the same golfer is having a particularly good round and is on track to score below 75, there is a heightened probability there will be a disaster on one hole towards the end of the round. This is due largely to the increased anxiety brought about by being outside one's comfort zone. This might be called a 'fear of success'. This anxiety will stop the golfer scoring better than their 'usual' result. Time and again we see a lesser ranked player fail after being in a winning position against a more highly fancied opponent. Some sports commentators refer to it as 'choking'. That is when a player is on the verge of a breakthrough win or result, they 'choke' and fail. This phenomenon occurs in all sports and across a wide range of athletes, from beginners to well-established performers. The choking arises because the player is outside their comfort zone and quite often also because the player loses concentration, as their thoughts turn to the result instead of focussing on the process.

Consider this next board where North-South were playing in the final of a major event for the first time. This is one circumstance which has frequently put players in all kinds of pursuits outside their comfort zone. After a pass by East, South made a highly aggressive pre-emptive three diamond bid at unfavourable vulnerability. West chose to make a take-out double rather than overcalling in spades and, sitting East, I elected to pass, hoping for a nice penalty.

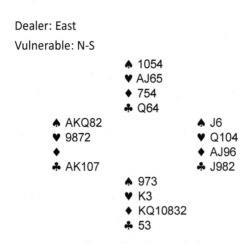

Dealer: East
Vulnerable: N-S

```
                    ♠ 1054
                    ♥ AJ65
                    ♦ 754
                    ♣ Q64
    ♠ AKQ82                    ♠ J6
    ♥ 9872                     ♥ Q104
    ♦                          ♦ AJ96
    ♣ AK107                    ♣ J982
                    ♠ 973
                    ♥ K3
                    ♦ KQ10832
                    ♣ 53
```

West began by cashing three rounds of spades before playing a top club. East showed an even number of clubs. After much thought West chose to switch to the nine of hearts covered by dummy's jack, queen and king leaving this position:

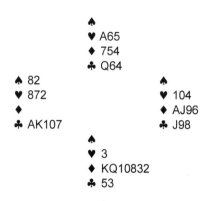

```
                    ♠
                    ♥ A65
                    ♦ 754
                    ♣ Q64
    ♠ 82                        ♠
    ♥ 872                       ♥ 104
    ♦                           ♦ AJ96
    ♣ AK107                     ♣ J98
                    ♠
                    ♥ 3
                    ♦ KQ10832
                    ♣ 53
```

Declarer lost the way a little now and tried a heart to dummy's ace and a heart return covered by East's ten and ruffed by declarer. Declarer continued with the five of clubs, won by West's king. When West exited with a club, declarer, who was left with only trumps, ruffed low and tried the king of diamonds. East made two further trump tricks, delivering North-South minus 800 on the board.

While some aggressive players might agree with South's decision to open three diamonds in second seat, it is clear that the decision is very marginal and one which might have come from being outside their comfort zone. Being outside your comfort zone can lead to mistakes occurring which might not otherwise happen. It could be the pressure of the situation got to South. Or the decision to bid may have come from prior experiences where they had been playing against weaker opposition and had not been penalised in similar circumstances. It is likely that the unfamiliar circumstances for North-South led to South making a bid which wasn't right for the situation.

Factors influencing our comfort zone

On many occasions we see players in all kinds of competitive events fail to surpass their previous results, despite having done very well in the early parts of their matches/tournaments. Comfort zones are not the only reason—sometimes it is fatigue or other factors at play. However, being outside the competitor's comfort zone can play a big part for many. The anxiety of being outside that zone is the main factor that causes the athlete to fail, assuming a comparative technical ability of the competitors.

In bridge, if we are used to running mid-field and all of a sudden we find ourselves in the lead, or playing the top team or pair, we are now outside our comfort zone. Our anxiety level may increase, and this may cause us to make errors that we would not make when playing against players at our 'usual' level, even if our skills or technical ability are sufficient. The comfort zone can also be at work when players start poorly and finish strongly.

Another factor which can play a part in determining our comfort zone is our environment. If we are playing a duplicate session at our club, we are more likely to be relaxed than if we are playing in a tournament where the environment is unfamiliar, the competition is different, the opponents are different and may play unfamiliar systems, and so on. Just like the tennis player who suddenly finds themselves playing on centre court, being outside your familiar environment may take you outside your comfort zone.

Many years ago when my partner and I were novices and found ourselves in the lead half-way through a tournament, we were dealt this board:

Dealer: East

Vulnerable: All

```
                        ♠ K98
                        ♥ A10743
                        ♦ 876
                        ♣ 92
        ♠ 754                       ♠ Q63
        ♥ 962                       ♥ J
        ♦ KJ42                      ♦ Q53
        ♣ J76                       ♣ K108543
                        ♠ AJ102
                        ♥ KQ85
                        ♦ A109
                        ♣ AQ
```

North	East	South	West
	Pass	2NT	Pass
3♥[1]	Pass	4♠[2]	Pass
4NT[3]	Pass	5♦[4]	Pass
6♥[5]	Pass	6♠[5]	All Pass

1 - Oops - do we play transfers over a strong 2NT?

2 - Super-accept for spades

3 - Keycard (1430), perhaps hoping partner would pass 4NT

4 - 0 or 3 keycards

5 - I really meant hearts as natural

6 - I want to protect my ♣AQ, so let's go with spades

We had managed to completely mess up the bidding to overbid to six spades, rather than the more logical six hearts. In fact, we shouldn't have been anywhere near the six level since any slam was pretty marginal. Despite being in the second-best contract—six spades is makeable by drawing three rounds of trumps finessing the queen of spades the right way, pitching a losing diamond on the long heart and finessing the king of clubs—sadly, our declarer play skills at the time weren't up to the challenge, and the loss of 11 IMPs on the board pushed us back into the middle of the field.

What happened on this hand? My partner and I were in a situation unfamiliar to us—leading an open event despite being very inexperienced players. Being outside our comfort zone is likely to have had an impact on our bidding and play on this hand. As novices we may have been expected to make some errors, but this hand was solvable for us since by recognising the bidding had gone off the rails, North could simply have passed four spades. However, the pressure of being outside our comfort zone could easily have been a contributing factor in our failure to get the best result.

Expanding your comfort zone

Breaking out of your comfort zone is one of the most difficult aspects any competitor contends with and being unable to do this is a significant factor in preventing competitors from achieving their goals, assuming skill and technical ability are sufficient. Unfortunately, there is no magic fix to adjusting your comfort zone. Lifting your comfort zone requires hard work and persistence over time. The first and most basic tenet is to make all your skills strong so that they will hold up under pressure and you don't make simple errors. A number of elements are involved and each must be addressed:

1. **Foster good habits during the card play.** For example, learn how to play basic card combinations, practice counting out the hand, and so on. Having practical habits such as counting tricks and points when dummy comes down means these abilities are more likely to hold up under pressure. The more automatic that these skills are, the greater your base skill level and the easier it will be to improve your comfort zone.

2. **Know your system 'inside out'.** Have strong system agreements and general principles that can be easily remembered (and which will apply in many auctions) to reduce the likelihood of errors when under pressure. Practicing your system using the 'partnership

bidding' feature on BBO[1] or uBid is also excellent for increasing system knowledge and comfort.

3. **Increase your exposure to being outside your comfort zone.** It's fair to say that the more frequently a player reaches the finals or plays in more difficult or competitive situations, the more likely they are to 'break through' and win. However, putting oneself in pressure situations by playing against stronger players, playing in a more competitive field, moving from the 'weak' side to the 'strong' side at your club, playing in open rather than restricted events and so on will also assist.

4. **Learn to maintain focus.** Keep your mind on playing or defending the current hand and don't be distracted by thoughts of winning or allow other factors like what is going on at the next table or what happened on the last hand to distract you from the task at hand. This will also help you ignore the setting which would otherwise take you out of your comfort zone. (Refer Chapter 4, page 65)

5. **Learn to relax at the table.** Some simple techniques to help you relax are described in the next chapter. It takes time and practice to acquire the ability to relax when under pressure. In the meantime, a few deep breaths will go a long way to helping you to relax at the table.

6. **Imagine yourself in situations outside your comfort zone.** Picturing yourself playing at table one in a Swiss event, or playing on vugraph or behind screens before you have to do it will help you to be prepared for the real thing. This is commonly known as visualisation in the sporting world and it can be of great assistance with improving your performance. There is more on visualisation and relaxation in the next chapter.

7. **Change your 'self-talk'.** Whenever you find yourself thinking or

---

1   BBO - Bridge Base Online is a free web-based computer application for bridge practice and play. Website: www.bridgebase.com
uBid is a partnership bidding app available for Android and Apple devices

saying a negative comment about your game, turn it into a positive one. For example, instead of saying "Oh, not another cross-ruff hand", say to yourself "I love the challenge of playing a cross-ruff hand".

The most important thing of all is believing you are good enough to win. If you believe that you are a good enough bridge player to win the match or tournament in which you are playing, your comfort zone will expand, the pressure you feel will be less, and your performance is likely to improve. Believing that you are good enough to win is likely to lead to you playing well enough to have a chance of winning—another example of a self-fulfilling prophecy.

Chapter 6

Relaxation and Mental Rehearsal

"A good athlete always mentally replays a competition over and over, even in victory, to see what might be done to improve the performance the next time."

- Frank Shorter, Olympic gold medallist, (marathon)

Over the years, players who have read my articles have often told me that they have struggled to get to sleep after playing bridge, particularly when they play at night. This is because their mind keeps re-playing the hands, a bid they made or didn't make, a signal from partner they missed or some other calamity that prevented them from meeting their goals. This concern is not uncommon to performers in all types of activities, whether it is athletes who may struggle to sleep properly on the night before a match due to pre-match excitement or a performer who is about to go on stage for the opening night at a concert. Pre- or post-match excitement and nerves affect players differently. Some thrive on it while others find their performance adversely affected by the inability to relax and switch off at the end of the day.

This is one hand where the decision that was made might cause a player to struggle to sleep:

Dealer: South

Vulnerable: All

```
                    ♠ Q754
                    ♥ K4
                    ♦ Q82
                    ♣ J954
      ♠ AK96                      ♠ 83
      ♥ AQ53                      ♥ 98762
      ♦ A9653                     ♦ K10
      ♣                           ♣ Q1076
                    ♠ J102
                    ♥ J10
                    ♦ J74
                    ♣ AK832
```

West	North	East	South
			Pass
1♦¹	Pass	Pass	2♣²
Dbl	3♣³	Pass	Pass
Dbl	All Pass		

1 - Promising five or more diamonds

2 - Balancing in the pass-out seat

3 - Let's try and prevent EW from getting back into the action

After the second take-out double, my partner sitting East chose to pass for penalties rather than bid their five-card heart suit which turned out to be a good decision for our side.

Sitting West I led the ace of spades (promising the king) on which East played the three of spades—upside down attitude, encouraging a continuation. The play continued with the king of spades followed by the six of spades for a ruff by partner asking for a diamond return. East now played the king of diamonds followed by a low diamond to my ace. I returned the nine of diamonds for a ruff (and asking for a heart return). After East returned a heart to my ace, declarer claimed the remaining six tricks for three off and -800.

On the lie of the cards East-West can make a small slam in hearts, but it is unlikely we would have reached that contract—some might not even reach game. North's bid of three clubs in an attempt to keep East out of the auction was a poor decision at this vulnerability despite compliance with the law of total tricks since South was a passed hand and North held such weak values.

With such a disastrous outcome from a marginal decision, at the end of the day, North might well continue to go over their decision to bid three clubs at the expense of much-needed relaxation for the next day.

It is not just poor decisions that can cause one to lose sleep. Often it is the situation one finds oneself in that preys on the mind at the end of the day.

Here's how the champion golfer Rory McIlroy described the circumstances around his implosion in the US Masters Golf tournament in 2011 when he was well in the lead going into the last round and poised to win his first major championship. In this excerpt from a newspaper article which quoted McIlroy's views on what happened, he describes how he turned his disappointment from this event into success in the next major event, just a few weeks later:[1]

"It was all about turning disappointment into motivation," he says. "I thought to myself, 'What I showed out there, that is not me. That is not who I want to be. I want to be a gritty competitor. I want to be able to close the deal. I don't want to crumble under pressure.' And I said to myself, 'I am never going to let that happen again.' I went home and analysed it. I watched the round on video. I talked to a few people... And I realised that I was way too focussed. I was thinking about the round overnight, during the morning; nothing else was on my mind. I was thinking about what could go right, but also about what could go wrong. I was too anxious and wound up. That is no state of mind in which to perform."

Two months later, he had a chance to deploy a different mental strategy when he led the US Open by eight shots going into the final

---

1   M Syed; The Times; June 13, 2015; Reprinted The Weekend Australian

day. Instead of agonising overnight about his final round, he switched off. "What I learnt from Augusta, and what I try to put into place every round now, is getting my mind away from the intensity and pressure. Even between shots, I have learnt to switch off. I talk to my caddie about a movie that I saw the night before, or a football match. Sometimes, I will tell JP [his caddie] to talk to me about a film, a match, anything to stop me focussing too hard.

Only as I approach the ball do I switch back on. This means there isn't enough time to think about what might go wrong, for negative thoughts, for doubts to creep into your mind. All you have time to do is to consider the shot in hand, pull the club from the bag, and visualise what you are going to do next. I am a very visual person: I create a picture of the flight of the ball, seeing in my mind what the ball is going to do. And then the final piece is to strike it."

From this excerpt it is clear that being extremely focussed can have drawbacks—it can lead to being 'wound up' and anxious. Being relaxed in sport and allowing the technique learnt through hours of practice to occur naturally is crucial for successful performance. There is a huge difference between planning during practice sessions what you will do when something goes wrong and thinking about what might happen endlessly on the night before your match.

While leading an event brings its own set of challenges for players, this article about McIlroy also brought to mind comments made to me by many bridge players regarding their continued thoughts about hands played (or perhaps misplayed) during the day or evening of bridge and the difficulty they have in switching off the mind. Constantly regurgitating the events of the day where things went wrong can be detrimental to a relaxed night and a good night's sleep leaving you tired for play the next day.

Similarly, checking out who you are playing the next day might also be a negative influence. For example, if you are an average player and are drawn to play the top seeded pair or a pair you dislike playing against in the next day's draw, how helpful is it for you to know that? Will you be more or less relaxed if you know the night before? Will you be better prepared knowing this? Will it prey on your mind if you know about it the night before? Would it be better to just look up your draw an hour before play and give the matter some thought at that time about how to prepare to play against that pair? Each person is different and while some will be unaffected by this type of information, others should give careful consideration to what they really need to know the night before a match.

What do you think and talk about during an event?

We have all heard comments like 'be positive' or 'think positively'. The reason for this is that the sub-conscious mind will move performance to whatever the conscious mind is thinking about.

» In shooting I always pictured the target and sight image that I wanted to have in my mind. I never pictured missing.

» A high jumper pictures themselves clearing the bar—they don't picture themselves hitting the bar.

» A tennis player pictures hitting the shot into the corner—they don't picture themselves missing or hitting it out.

» A basketball player pictures being at the free throw line and throwing the ball through the hoop—they don't picture the ball bouncing off the rim.

Having an image of the desired outcome is an important factor in success.

During my shooting career, I was often asked about the shot(s) that I had missed and what had happened. Seriously? How does it help someone to know why I missed a shot? Wouldn't it be better to know how I got 59 out of 60 shots right, rather than to know about the one that was imperfect?

Similarly, in bridge the hand reviews at score-up and over lunch or dinner often focus on the area where the pair lost the most points. It is common in score-ups to hear players ask "What happened on board 7?" or "How did they make game there?". This will generally be the board where you have lost points. You hardly ever hear players saying "Wow! That was a great result. How did you make that game/slam?"

I am not suggesting you should never review your performance and analyse what you could have done better, but this review is often best done at a training session or after play is over for the day rather than during the event. Focussing on the positives and what you do well during a match can make a huge difference to your confidence and your mental approach at the table.

The following hand gained our side a great result when North chose to pass and play in 3NT, rather than bidding four hearts which risks going one off. It is often said that nine tricks are easier than ten, and that certainly proved true here:

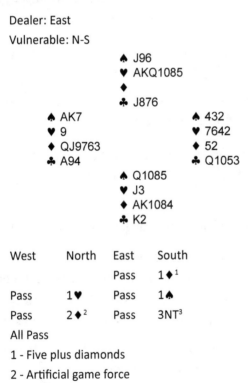

Dealer: East
Vulnerable: N-S

```
                      ♠ J96
                      ♥ AKQ1085
                      ♦
                      ♣ J876
        ♠ AK7                      ♠ 432
        ♥ 9                        ♥ 7642
        ♦ QJ9763                   ♦ 52
        ♣ A94                      ♣ Q1053
                      ♠ Q1085
                      ♥ J3
                      ♦ AK1084
                      ♣ K2
```

West	North	East	South
		Pass	1♦[1]
Pass	1♥	Pass	1♠
Pass	2♦[2]	Pass	3NT[3]
All Pass			

1 - Five plus diamonds
2 - Artificial game force

3 - Minimum hand to play. Denies three hearts. Note that some pairs might by agreement bid two hearts over the game-forcing two diamonds to show two card support, and three hearts to show three card support.

Opposite a hand that had shown five diamonds as well as values in clubs, North chose to pass three no-trumps rather than risk losing four tricks in four hearts. Three no-trumps by South is untouchable on correct play as spades can easily be set up for the extra tricks.

Four hearts looks like it has good chances, but our teammates found the killing defence by leading a spade to the king, cashing the spade ace and exiting a third spade. Even after declarer takes two discards on the top diamonds, there is no way to avoid losing two clubs with the ace off-side.

A hand like this where both tables do something good and it ends up being worth twelve IMPs to your team is worth focussing on. This is the sort of hand which can give your team confidence by talking about it, rather than grinding over the hands where you lost IMPs.

A few years ago, I gave one of my first talks on mental management to some members of the Australian bridge team. I suggested to them the importance of focussing on their good boards during the score-up and providing positive feedback to each other on their successes. A few months later, some of those players were part of a team at the Australian Summer Festival of Bridge which is one of the major events on the Australian domestic calendar. One of the team had told me they had decided during this event to adopt this approach and no matter what went wrong they were only going to talk about their good boards at score up. Despite a disastrous start, he told me they had stayed committed to this approach and reached the finals of the Seniors' event, eventually winning the trophy.

While the importance of end of day/match review of hands where mistakes were made with your partner should not be underestimated, consider how often you review and discuss the hands where things went right with your partner. How much better will you feel going into your next match when you know you got lots of things right in the last match? Try adopting a positive approach and focus on the hands where things went right—whether it was a perfectly bid slam, or a good part-score result or a nice piece of defence. Finish your daily review at the end of play on a high note, relax and enjoy your evening.

Taking this positive thought with you to bed is more likely to give you a better mindset for the next day of bridge and a better night's sleep, than if you spent the evening worrying about a hand you messed up or one on which your partner made a mistake. You cannot change the result of that hand and compounding the error you made by dwelling on it is unlikely to lead to an improved performance the next day. As in sport, having a mental picture of a great result, a well-played hand or an elegant bidding sequence is more likely to lead to a strong performance in your next day's matches rather than the converse. I am sure we have all encountered auctions like the one on this delightful hand played in a teams' event:

Dealer: South
Vulnerable: N-S

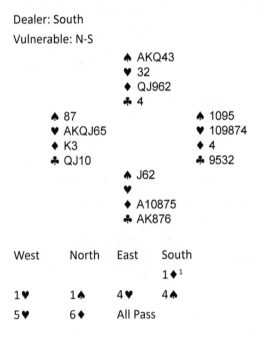

West	North	East	South
			1♦[1]
1♥	1♠	4♥	4♠
5♥	6♦	All Pass	

1 - Promises at least a five-card suit

West's five heart bid created a difficult decision for me sitting North, as I had to decide between six diamonds, five spades or double. The possibility of a grand slam was also lurking. As things stood, I decided six diamonds was the safest contract. It seemed likely we were missing an ace and with our ten-card fit a diamond ruff at trick one was possible if we played in spades. On the lead of the ace of hearts, twelve tricks are made with declarer losing only the diamond king.

Our teammates brought back a score of -200 when the opposing side failed to double five hearts after the following auction.

West	North	East	South
			1♦[1]
2♥[2]	2♠	3♠[3]	4♠
Pass	Pass	5♥	All Pass

1 - Better minor
2 - Intermediate jump with six hearts
3 - 'Good' raise to four hearts or stopper ask

North-South were clearly misled by East's inventive three spade bid. Nevertheless, North's decision to pass rather than double five hearts was a little timid and resulted in a big pickup for our team.

When you make the correct decision on this type of auction by bidding six diamonds or by misleading the opponents with a sneaky bid it helps to build confidence. When something has worked well for you, finishing your end of day post-mortem by talking about it will go a long way towards building your confidence for the next day's play. Additionally, knowing that your system agreement is delivering good results for you builds confidence, particularly when you consider what might have occurred had you been using an alternative system structure.

Using relaxation to switch off

Even with a positive outlook, the excitement or disappointment of competition might still make getting a good night's rest difficult. Learning how to relax the body and clear the mind in order to get a decent night's sleep, particularly in a multi-day competition, is a skill that can be learnt just like any other skill associated with playing bridge. More importantly, developing the ability to relax can help you reduce anxiety in a match simply by taking a couple of deep breaths—a skill that athletes use in competition to great effect. Relaxation is also used as a preparatory step for mental rehearsal which is discussed later in this chapter.

There are many different relaxation methodologies available such as progressive relaxation, breathing techniques, meditation and so on.

The technique that I liked to use when I was competing in shooting, and which has been widely used at high level sport, is known as autogenic training. This technique uses relaxation to prepare the mind for mental rehearsal and it has been proven to be very effective in this regard. Autogenic training creates a perception of heaviness and warmth in the body to create a state of enhanced relaxation which is more conducive to learning skills. The player who practices this technique can also quickly return to a relaxed state when they are in a stressful situation, such as in competition, enabling the player to focus and overcome distractions.

Over 3,000 clinical studies have shown autogenic training (which originated in Germany in 1932 by Dr Johannes Schultz) to be effective in many areas including:

» enhancing performance;

» assisting memory and focus;

» inducing a feeling of well-being and confidence;

» improving the quality of sleep.

It takes at least 2 - 3 months to become accustomed to the autogenic training technique, but I believe spending 15 minutes on this every night until it becomes second nature will assist you in the long run.

Over time your body and mind will learn to respond to the relaxation procedure and you will reach the point where you can relax quickly. With daily practice you will eventually be able to achieve a level of relaxation by simply taking a few deep breaths. Relaxation techniques such as this are usually used as a precursor to mental rehearsal so that 5-10 minutes is spent on relaxation followed by 10-20 minutes for the rehearsal. Being in a relaxed state prior to rehearsal will make the rehearsal more effective, since brains in a relaxed state are better able to remember new information.[2]

After reading one of my articles on relaxation where I mentioned this technique, a bridge player asked me if I would send them more details on autogenic training. A few weeks later, I saw the player at an event. She told me that she wished she had heard about this method 20 years ago as she had found using the technique really helped her get a good night's sleep.

The internet offers a wide variety of information on this and other relaxation techniques. I have also included a general script on autogenic training in Appendix 1 to give you a feel for the technique. If you are interested in this technique, I encourage you to flip to the back of the book now and read through the detailed description.

For those of you who want something that you can start straight away, I have outlined in the box on the next page a simple relaxation technique to use.

---

2   Nature Journal, 2010

Technical Excerpt - Relaxation Technique

The following script can be put on to a tape or learnt and then followed (proceed slowly allowing at least five to ten minutes for the relaxation exercise).

Settle yourself into a comfortable seated position. Adjust your posture so that the chair is completely supporting your weight. Close your eyes and begin by taking three long, slow breaths, focussing on the feeling of relaxation each time as you breathe out. Notice with each breath that you take that there is a moment of relief with the exhalation of each breath.

Continue to breathe slowly, enjoying the feeling of relaxation and as you do try to associate that pleasant feeling with an increasing heaviness in each muscle group within your body.

Let that feeling begin in the muscles around your forehead and face and then let it spread very slowly down through your neck and shoulders. Continue the spread of relaxation taking at least two minutes to spread it down through your whole body.

When you have relaxed each and every muscle group within your body, take two more deep breaths and enjoy the feeling of relaxation.

If you are combining relaxation with mental rehearsal, you would start your rehearsal and visualisation at this point.

When you wish to 're-awaken' count slowly backwards from 5 to 1 stretching your muscles as you do so. You will then feel refreshed and rested. (Naturally you will skip this step if you are doing this at night in bed and want to fall asleep).

Being able to relax and focus was of great assistance to me when I needed to be able to think clearly to ensure the correct approach was taken to make my Moysian four heart contract on this deal:

Dealer: East
Vulnerable: All

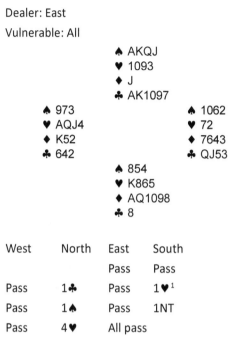

West	North	East	South
		Pass	Pass
Pass	1♣	Pass	1♥[1]
Pass	1♠	Pass	1NT
Pass	4♥	All pass	

1 - Walsh style preference, bidding a major ahead of diamonds

West chose to lead the seven of spades and on seeing dummy, my first reaction was to wonder about North's decision to bid four hearts instead of perhaps three hearts, or two diamonds, fourth-suit-forcing. With such a great diamond suit in the South hand, three no-trumps appeared at first glance to be a better contract. As it turned out, on the lie of the cards four hearts or four spades are both makeable double dummy whereas three no-trumps is doomed with insufficient entries to the South hand.

Thoughts about what bid partner could have made might sometimes be unavoidable, but they are distracting and likely to increase tension. So I took a deep breath to relax and clear my mind, said my cue word to myself and focussed on the best line of play to make this difficult contract.

(hand repeated below)

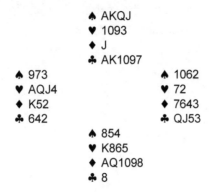

```
              ♠ AKQJ
              ♥ 1093
              ♦ J
              ♣ AK1097
♠ 973                      ♠ 1062
♥ AQJ4                     ♥ 72
♦ K52                      ♦ 7643
♣ 642                      ♣ QJ53
              ♠ 854
              ♥ K865
              ♦ AQ1098
              ♣ 8
```

Holding such poor trumps, the best choice appeared to be to play the hand on a cross ruff. I won the spade lead in dummy, crossed to the ace of diamonds and ruffed a diamond with both opponents following. I then continued with the ace and king of clubs pitching a diamond, followed by a club ruff in hand. I ruffed a third diamond and when West followed with the king of diamonds, I cashed two spades in dummy. When these held, I was already up to nine tricks and when I could ruff a club low in my hand, West could over-ruff but had to give me the king of hearts for my tenth trick.

The above hand was complex and required full concentration to have a good chance of success. Extraneous thoughts about partner's choices would have been at best unhelpful since these interfere with your focus and concentration. Being able to relax and re-focus so that distracting thoughts about the auction do not interfere with your play is an important skill for the bridge player to learn. Autogenic training is one technique which will assist with acquiring this skill.

Mental Rehearsal (Visualisation)

Mental rehearsal involves visualising in your mind either the environment you are going to be performing in or the actual skill/performance you are about to execute prior to the event. We have all heard people say things like "I was a bit nervous playing on centre court for the first time", or "I was a bit nervous playing the top seeds", or "I was a bit nervous being in the final". I stated previously, anxiety associated with performing in an unfamiliar or high-pressure environment is often the reason why people fail at the task they are trying to perform—even when they have the necessary technical skills and ability to succeed. Mental rehearsal can assist with overcoming this nervousness and allow you to perform as you would if no-one was watching and nothing was at stake. Additionally, mental rehearsal helps you to perfect a skill more quickly than just practicing the skill alone.

Athletes, business people, fighter pilots, doctors and people in all types of professions use mental rehearsal and visualisation to help them achieve successful performances during the activity. For example:

» Professional basketball players may mentally picture themselves shooting the ball through the basket from the free throw line before making the throw in a match. They will think about how the shot feels based on a shot they have executed previously in practice or a match.

» A guest speaker who gets nervous when presenting may use mental rehearsal to picture giving the speech in the auditorium.

» Golfers will visualise the shot they want to hit and take some practice swings before they step up to the ball to hit the shot.

» High jumpers will picture themselves taking their run up and clearing the bar before they make their attempt.

» A surgeon may mentally rehearse executing a complex procedure before actually performing the operation.

» Athletes in Olympic and other events obtain photos of the competition arena prior to their event so that they can familiarise themselves with the field of play prior to their match.

Being mentally comfortable and prepared helps the athlete or performer to execute the task at hand. Studies have shown that the mind cannot tell the difference between a real performance and an imagined performance.[3] It has also been shown that people will improve a skill more quickly using a combination of mental rehearsal and practice than simply using practice alone. While these studies have generally been related to activities requiring motor skills, there seems to me to be no reason why the same will not hold true for a mental game like bridge.

If a player visualises a skill they want to improve over and over using mental rehearsal, they will improve that skill faster than by simply practicing the skill during training. The mind knows what to expect in the situation so that the focus of the individual is on the performance, rather than the circumstances, the environment or other factors.

How could mental rehearsal help a bridge player?

Let's consider a really basic example to illustrate this. You hold:

♠ AJx ♥ xxx ♦ QJxx ♣ xxx

Playing Standard American you hear your partner open one heart, and the opponents overcall two clubs.

» If you are an experienced player you will bid two hearts without much thought, since as an experienced player you have encountered this situation many times before. It requires no mental energy and your skill level is such that you know the response automatically.

» If you are a new player, you might find you have to think about what you have been taught to do in this situation. You might have to take your time to remember your notes. The response is not automatic, because the technical skill is not yet embedded for you.

---

3   Mental Representation and Mental Practice: Experimental Investigation on the Functional Links between Motor Memory and Motor Imagery; Cornelia Frank, William M. Land, Carmen Popp, and Thomas Schack; Published: April 17, 2014. https://doi.org/10.1371/journal.pone.0095175

If as a new player you mentally practiced this sequence with slight variations such as with and without interference, but with the same type of hand, you would reach the level where this bid required minimal effort much faster than if you only practiced this bidding sequence once a week at the bridge club.

Those of us who have observed newer players at the club will have noticed how much effort they have to put into their decisions and how mentally exhausted they can be at the end of a session. The more experienced we are and the more practice we have done on specific situations, the more likely we are to successfully navigate those specific situations in competitions.

The use of mental rehearsal and visualisation in sport and the other situations I have described is well established. In considering how these same methods might be applied to assist with improving your play at bridge, I believe there are several more areas where mental rehearsal could be effective. These are:

Card combinations:

Rehearsal could be useful to practice the play of specific card combinations when you want to learn the percentage line to take to make the most tricks or a specific number of tricks.

For example, mentally rehearse the lines you would take to play the following holdings:

AKQ10	v	xxx	for 4 tricks
	or		
AQ10xx	v	xxxx	for 5 tricks
	or		
AJxx	v	K9xx	for 3 tricks

The number of card combinations is quite extensive, but many combinations come up quite frequently and knowing how to get these right every time will help in pressure situations.

Environment:

Every player experiences aspects of bridge for the first time. It might be your first club competition, congress, major tournament or state trial. It could be your first time behind screens, the first time you have played in a major event, the first time you have played on vugraph[4], or just the first time you have a kibitzer sitting at your table and watching you play.

Some players will be unaffected by the 'new' experience, while others might perform below their best due to the unfamiliar environment. Using mental rehearsal prior to the event to visualise yourself in that environment before you experience it live can help you to be more comfortable with the environment with which you are going to be faced, if and when it happens.

Learning conventions:

Some players often have difficulty remembering a convention they have agreed to play with their partner or that is new to them. Using visualisation to rehearse the bidding sequences where that convention will apply will assist with ensuring the convention will be remembered in the match environment.

Bidding sequences:

You could use rehearsal to visualise particular hands you are dealt and practice your responses as if your partner had opened the bidding.

Play skills:

---

4   Vugraph is a tournament display program which is used to broadcast bridge events, either to an onsite theatre, or online, sometimes to thousands of kibitzers. These days the most common place to watch it is on Bridge Base Online.

Picturing the layout of the hands and then the mechanics of the skill you are trying to consolidate e.g. executing a squeeze, endplaying an opponent, counting the hand during play, etc.

Common occurrences:

Rehearsal can also be useful to deal with certain environmental occurrences that inhibit performance. Different things affect different people, but if the player is aware of their personal negative influences (e.g. chatty opponents, noisy room, director calls, etc.), then mental rehearsal can help prepare a structured response to these occurrences.

One of these common occurrences, which I am sure we have all encountered, is hesitations during bidding. Rehearsing how you will deal with the opponent's hesitation is important to ensure your side is not damaged:

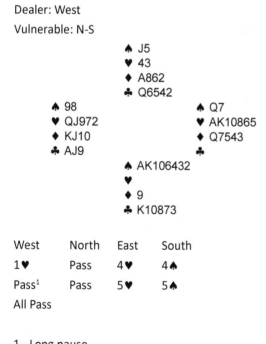

Dealer: West
Vulnerable: N-S

```
                    ♠ J5
                    ♥ 43
                    ♦ A862
                    ♣ Q6542
        ♠ 98                    ♠ Q7
        ♥ QJ972                 ♥ AK10865
        ♦ KJ10                  ♦ Q7543
        ♣ AJ9                   ♣
                    ♠ AK106432
                    ♥
                    ♦ 9
                    ♣ K10873
```

West	North	East	South
1♥	Pass	4♥	4♠
Pass[1]	Pass	5♥	5♠
All Pass			

1 - Long pause

East's four heart bid, while not everyone's choice, was certainly effective on this board. South had an easy four spade bid, but West then went into the tank before passing. With extreme shape and no defence against four spades, East decided to bid on. The director may have had a tricky ruling if five spades had failed and if East had a more marginal bid after West's hesitation.

Before play commenced, South quietly made mention of the pause in the bidding tempo before West's pass, and all players agreed that this had occurred. Five spades made twelve tricks on the heart lead (after the opponents helped out with the club suit) and there was no need to involve the director. Interestingly, at favourable vulnerability, six hearts would have been an excellent save over the making five spade contract. (Note: even at equal vulnerability, six hearts would be a good save.)

The final contract making is not always what happens and having planned what you will do if and when these circumstances arise will assist in ensuring you manage these situations effectively. You should also rehearse what you will do if your partner hesitates and the opponents make mention of this.

Visualisation and rehearsal may be used to help with any aspect of your game that you want to improve, and it is particularly helpful with ensuring you are prepared for all the common occurrences which arise at the bridge table.

How to rehearse effectively

The first step is to achieve a state of relaxation using one of the methods described in this chapter. Next, rehearse the aspect of your performance you want to work on. It may be picturing yourself playing on vugraph. It might be the start of the match where you see yourself and your partner at the table bidding and playing the first few hands. It might be picturing a hand and bidding a particular convention. Whichever aspect you choose to rehearse, try to make the rehearsal as real as possible. For example, if you decide to rehearse playing the first few hands, in order to make the rehearsal as real as possible, consider the following aspects:

» Picture yourself at the table with your partner and opponents (it doesn't really matter who the opponents are, but don't use the same people every time);

» Picture yourself picking your hand up and counting the cards and sorting them;

» Imagine the hand you have been dealt, count your points;

» Imagine your partner opening the bidding and writing their bid (or using a bidding box);

» Imagine yourself making your response;

» Imagine you are declarer in the final contract;

» Imagine partner's hand coming down and the cards being exactly what you expected;

» Imagine playing the hand;

» Imagine making your contract and the feeling of satisfaction that you have got off to a good start in the tournament;

» Repeat for the next hand.

Rehearse one skill or aspect per rehearsal session. You can repeat a skill in several rehearsal sessions until you feel comfortable that you have mastered it. Thousands of athletes have found that spending 20 minutes a day on relaxation and mental rehearsal is worth the effort. Mental rehearsal cannot replace practical training, but used in conjunction, it can enhance your ability as a player.

Chapter 7

Stopping Negative Thinking

"If we all did the things we are capable of doing, we would literally astound ourselves."

- Thomas Alva Edison, inventor and scientist

"I hate playing in no-trumps."

"I don't play well against Fred and Joe."

I am sure we have all heard comments like this from many players. Some of us say things like this to ourselves. This self-talk is the running commentary we have inside our heads. Whether you say it or simply think it, the effect on your mind is the same. A key issue for many competitors is the little voice inside their head that prevents that competitor from winning. That little voice is usually accompanied by negative thinking that can destroy confidence and lead to poor performance.

The negative inner voice creates doubt in many different circumstances for competitors in all sports and activities. In high jumping it might be: "I've missed this height in the past". In shooting it might be "I always miss my last shot" or "I always miss my first shot", while in running it might be "I'd better not miss the start". The 'not' word or its various facsimiles stick in the mind which only tends to focus on the 'miss the start' part and ignores the 'not' word.

In shooting sports, a lot of competitors struggled when it was windy. I generally loved shooting when it was windy and won my individual gold medal at the Commonwealth Games in relatively windy conditions. I liked shooting in these conditions because I always felt like I had an advantage since so many shooters were very negative about it. Essentially, they talked themselves out of doing well before they even started the match. When I saw the windy conditions in Manchester at the 2002 Commonwealth Games, I was ready for them.

Comments heard around the shooting range on windy days were reflective of many competitors' negative thoughts about the conditions and their past performances in those conditions. Shooters would often talk themselves into believing that the conditions were more difficult than they really were. Even better, the opponents would tell other competitors how hard the conditions were! By doing this they weren't just affecting their own confidence with these comments—they were also helping their competitors lose confidence. A more positive way of dealing with a windy day would be to realise that the conditions are difficult for everyone and to use some positive commentary or thoughts about a previous good performance in those conditions to generate some confidence and self-belief.

It seems that this type of negative attitude is alive and well at bridge events. I recall a recent occasion when I was playing at a tournament where the lighting conditions were not the best. A number of players seemed to be allowing these conditions to interfere with their concentration. Instead of focussing and concentrating harder on the hand being played to avoid making a careless error, the comments about the bad light were prevalent. In these conditions, reaching four spades on the following hand provided a challenge for my declarer play:

Dealer: East

Vulnerable: N-S

```
                        ♠ 2
                        ♥ K6
                        ♦ AJ1085
                        ♣ KJ872
        ♠ KQ763                         ♠
        ♥ AQ8                           ♥ 975432
        ♦ 92                            ♦ KQ73
        ♣ 965                           ♣ 1043
                        ♠ AJ109854
                        ♥ J10
                        ♦ 64
                        ♣ AQ
```

West	North	East	South
		Pass	1♠
Pass	2♦	Pass	4♠
All Pass			

When partner put dummy down after West's lead of the nine of diamonds, I could see a couple of potential issues with this contract. It looked like West's lead was from either a singleton or doubleton, so placing West with longer trumps looked right. With one heart to lose if the suit could be correctly guessed, it seemed to me that the main danger was that trumps might break badly. I had to hope that the clubs were breaking so I could ditch my losing diamond too.

After winning the lead with the ace, I began by playing the ace of clubs, overtaking the queen of clubs with the king and discarding my diamond loser on the jack of clubs, both defenders following. Now I tried dummy's jack of diamonds which was covered by East's queen and ruffed by my four of spades with West following suit.

It might have been tempting to exit with a spade at this point. However, that would lead to the loss of an extra spade trick in the end game.

The correct line was to play a heart which West ducked and I won with dummy's king and exited with a heart, won by West's queen, leaving this position:

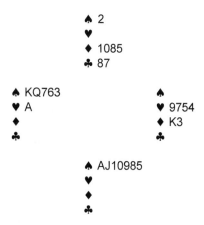

```
            ♠ 2
            ♥
            ♦ 1085
            ♣ 87

♠ KQ763              ♠
♥ A                  ♥ 9754
♦                    ♦ K3
♣                    ♣

            ♠ AJ10985
            ♥
            ♦
            ♣
```

West is now endplayed. If West plays a heart, declarer ruffs low and can now only lose two spade tricks. If West exits a spade declarer can win and can exit with a spade which places West back in the same dilemma.

If I had played a spade earlier (before playing a heart), West could have won and played ace and another heart to dummy. Whatever I play off the dummy, West can either overruff low or discard when I ruff with an intermediate to build a fourth trick.

The theme of this hand is the same as many throughout this book: bridge is a complex game, and it is hard to perform complex tasks if internal or external factors are distracting you. If I had allowed myself to be distracted by thoughts about the poor lighting rather than the task at hand, it is unlikely I would have succeeded in four spades.

Being able to focus and maintain concentration despite poor playing conditions is critical to success. Instead of allowing the bad light to distract you, a good player will mentally say—"The low light doesn't bother me. I can still see the cards okay. It will give me an advantage because everyone else is going to be distracted by this."

The negative 'little voice' inside your head

The common 'little voice' phrase in bridge goes something like "I hate playing in 1NT", and after you have gone one off saying to yourself (or aloud), "I always mess up one no-trump contracts". When you fail, the little voice says "yep, that is just like me, I always mess up one no-trump". This type of reflective comment simply reinforces in your mind the negative thinking and increases the likelihood of failing the next time. A negative mindset does nothing to help you make your contract.

Some players will go so far as to create an 'excuse' for themselves to fail. This could be staying out late the night before a match, over-indulging in alcohol or simply making out that they feel unwell before the event starts. When and if they perform poorly, they can drag out the 'excuse' like "I wasn't feeling well", or "I had a late night", etc. These people are really just giving themselves an 'out' ahead of time. They 'think' they might not do well, so they create an excuse ahead of the performance. Even worse is where a player sees dummy come down and instead of thanking partner and working out how to make the contract, they focus on how bad things look. Consider this deal:

Dealer: North
Vulnerable: N-S

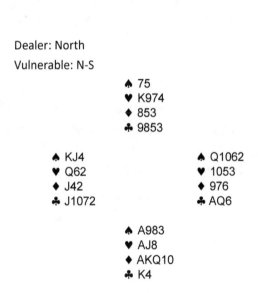

```
                  ♠ 75
                  ♥ K974
                  ♦ 853
                  ♣ 9853

    ♠ KJ4                      ♠ Q1062
    ♥ Q62                      ♥ 1053
    ♦ J42                      ♦ 976
    ♣ J1072                    ♣ AQ6

                  ♠ A983
                  ♥ AJ8
                  ♦ AKQ10
                  ♣ K4
```

We had an auction where my strong two no-trump opening as South was raised to three no-trumps by my partner. It would have been easy for me to be negative about this hand with only seven top tricks obvious after the lead of the two of clubs from West. However, I kept a positive mindset and thought about what needed to happen to make the contract, rather than the fact that it looked like it was doomed.

I decided the contract would make if the stars aligned for me. Diamonds had to be 3-3, or the jack dropping in one or two rounds. Hearts had to be 3-3, or I had to find a singleton queen or ten. Finally, I wanted East to return a club after winning with the ace of clubs as clubs looked to be 4-3 from the opening lead. I didn't want to deal with a switch to a spade at trick two if that suit was breaking 5-2.

My wishes were granted as East returned a club to my king at trick two. I played the ace of hearts then ducked a heart to East, who won with the ten and switched to a diamond. I rose with the ace of diamonds before playing the jack of hearts and was quite relieved to see this covered by the queen allowing me to wrap up nine tricks when diamonds also broke 3-3.

It is easy to become negative when things don't look good. Focussing attention on negative elements – 'this is a bad contract; partner made a bad bid; this result will badly affect our score'– only distracts from the task at hand. As can be seen from this example, thinking about what has to happen or be right for a contract to make, rather than worrying about how bad the contract is, will be more likely to deliver a positive outcome for your side.

In addition, poor or (seemingly) hopeless contracts can be a chance to shine. Instead of approaching the hand negatively, a player might think, "This contract looks tough. Wouldn't it be wonderful if I could find a way to make it?". In fact, great players look for a chance to make this type of contract by an end play or squeeze so they can talk to others about how they managed to make the seemingly impossible contract.

Overcoming negative thoughts and actions is critical to successful performance. Approaching the competition and each hand with optimism is not always enough. A life-time of the 'little voice' can be hard to overcome. Even those players who enter a match with an initial positive focus might find that after one or two perceived 'bad' boards, the 'little voice' has re-appeared, creating doubt and loss of confidence. These players often find themselves in a mid-match slump from which recovery is impossible. It should be clear if this is happening to you that finding a solution for the negative inner voice is worth considering.

Imagine that cross-ruffing a hand is not one of your strengths and you become declarer in four hearts on the following deal:

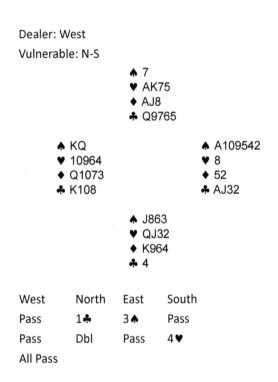

Dealer: West
Vulnerable: N-S

	♠ 7	
	♥ AK75	
	♦ AJ8	
	♣ Q9765	

♠ KQ		♠ A109542
♥ 10964		♥ 8
♦ Q1073		♦ 52
♣ K108		♣ AJ32

	♠ J863	
	♥ QJ32	
	♦ K964	
	♣ 4	

West	North	East	South
Pass	1♣	3♠	Pass
Pass	Dbl	Pass	4♥
All Pass			

As dummy comes down a positive thought like—"Great! Looks like I need to cross-ruff this hand to make ten tricks. It's good to have a chance to put my recent training into practice at the table."—before playing to trick one will go a long way to helping your confidence and helping you to focus on the right line.

On the lead of the king of spades you can see that the diamond finesse probably needs to be working and that East's pre-emptive three spades might mean trumps are breaking badly. At trick two, West attempted to cut down declarer's ruffing potential by continuing with a low heart won in dummy with the king of hearts. Clearing the way for a cross-ruff, declarer switched to a low club won by East's jack. It would have been better to let West win the trick to play another trump. East exited with the five of diamonds to West's queen and dummy's ace—who said the opponents aren't allowed to help you out sometimes by giving you a free finesse!

Declarer now played the seven of clubs ruffed in hand followed by a spade ruff in dummy. With seven trump tricks available (one on West's trump switch and six ruffs), declarer needs three diamond tricks to bring the total to ten. It is best to cash these immediately before West can discard diamonds on spade ruffs. There is a good indication that East won't ruff in since East didn't return a trump after winning the club trick. After declarer cashes the jack and king of diamonds, cross-ruffing the rest of the hand leads to a painless ten tricks.

The way to play the hand simply required logical thought as long as declarer kept the goal in sight and thought positively. Allowing extraneous thoughts such as "I find cross-ruffing hands really difficult" were more likely to be distracting and lead declarer astray.

Some players may find that simply being made aware of this tendency will enable them to change negative statements into positive sentiments. Replacing negative thoughts "I hate playing in one no-trump" with a positive thought "I always play well in one no-trump" will help get you in the right frame of mind to succeed.

However, some players might need a process in addition to using positive commentary such as "I can make one no-trump", or "I can beat this pair" to help stop these negative thoughts. One option sometimes used is known as 'the rubber band' method, which is outlined at the end of this chapter.

The concept of 'thought-stopping' for negative thoughts ("I always go off in one no-trump") followed by a positive thought ("I can make one no-trump") should mean that over time your negative thoughts lessen. After a period of time you will find you have no negative thoughts and you can stop wearing the rubber band.

You will find that stopping negative thinking will be instrumental in improving your overall performance and assisting in your success at the bridge table.

Technical Excerpt

This technique is suggested as a mechanism to stop negative thinking which some players may find helpful.

Rubber Band Method for Stopping Negative Thinking

1. List at least five types of negative thoughts that commonly occur to you in bridge.

2. Put a rubber band (or wrist band) around your wrist that fits snugly and which can snap. Wear it all day every day. Choose something that you feel comfortable wearing around. (Note if you feel uncomfortable wearing something like this all the time, you could choose to wear it during play and score-up sessions).

3. Whenever you are aware of negative thoughts, the band should be pulled and released so that it stings your wrist. This means you are introducing a circuit-breaker or distraction for yourself from a negative thought. It is a 'thought-stopping' procedure.

4. After each time you have flicked the rubber band, execute a positive thought relating to the same situation. So if the thought that occurred was "I always mess up at.....", change the thought to "I usually succeed at.....".

Chapter 8

Goal Setting and Performance Evaluation

"You have to set goals that are almost out of reach. If you set a goal that is attainable without much thought, you are stuck with something below your true talent and potential."

- Steve Garvey, leading American baseball player

Most of us like to do well at our chosen game. Whether one competes for fun, social or competitive reasons, there are very few people who play competitive games who are happy when they lose. While it is true there are some who consider the social aspect as important, if not more important, than winning, most like to do well.

If you like to play for fun and enjoy a social day out at the club without worrying too much about your results, then goal setting may not be something you want to spend time on and you might want to skip this chapter.

If, however, you aspire to improve and to win, then having goals will be an important part of managing both your improvement strategy and your mental approach to the game. Goals also help you to manage your expectations. Knowing that your plan is working and that you are on track towards achieving your goals will assist with your self-belief and help prevent doubt and negative thinking in competition. Regardless of your motivation for playing bridge, setting some basic goals will help you to improve at the game.

Most people will be familiar with score-based goals. The more competitive amongst us usually have some score type goals in competition; e.g. finishing in the top ten, beating a particular pair at the local club, getting over 70% in a matchpoint game, attaining a certain masterpoint rank, and so on. The better you are at the game, the more ambitious your score goals are likely to be.

A simple kind of goal that some players might have is to improve their play on a particular type of hand. For example, imagine that improving your squeeze play is an area you want to improve to take your playing ability to the next level. In order to do this, you need to practice playing these types of hands.

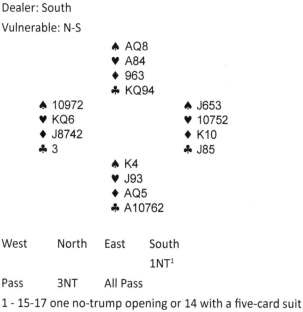

Dealer: South
Vulnerable: N-S

	♠ AQ8	
	♥ A84	
	♦ 963	
	♣ KQ94	
♠ 10972		♠ J653
♥ KQ6		♥ 10752
♦ J8742		♦ K10
♣ 3		♣ J85
	♠ K4	
	♥ J93	
	♦ AQ5	
	♣ A10762	

West	North	East	South
			1NT[1]
Pass	3NT	All Pass	

1 - 15-17 one no-trump opening or 14 with a five-card suit

On the lead of the four of diamonds declarer can immediately see eleven tricks. Finding the twelfth trick required the right conditions for a squeeze in the end game.

West's diamond lead was won by declarer, with East playing the king. Declarer played three rounds of clubs ending in hand before cashing the king of spades and continuing with the nine of hearts won by West's queen and ducked by dummy leaving this position (the East hand is irrelevant to the squeeze).

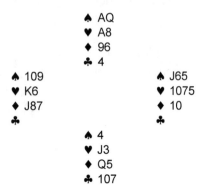

```
                    ♠ AQ
                    ♥ A8
                    ♦ 96
                    ♣ 4
    ♠ 109                         ♠ J65
    ♥ K6                          ♥ 1075
    ♦ J87                         ♦ 10
    ♣                             ♣
                    ♠ 4
                    ♥ J3
                    ♦ Q5
                    ♣ 107
```

When West now exited with a diamond, declarer won in hand before cashing two spades, both defenders following. Now declarer returned to hand with a club to cash the remaining two clubs. On the last club West was squeezed and had to choose between discarding the winning diamond or baring his king of hearts.

While only gaining an extra IMP for our side, it was nevertheless a nice play and one which came from practicing these types of plays with a computer program on squeeze play. If your goal is to improve at squeeze play, this hand changes from a boring hand with two overtricks to a challenge worth your effort. It is also worth remembering in pairs competition, the extra trick can mean a massive percentage boost in your score. Finally, occasionally you will find yourself in slam where making the twelfth trick is essential, so practicing this skill is worthwhile.

In bridge we are fortunate to have so many wonderful computer programs to assist with learning these types of skills. An excellent resource to improve your technical skills is the Bridge Master deals, available through Bridge Base Online. If computer programs are not your thing, then you might consider taking some lessons.

Set yourself goals

As an international athlete, I always had goals for both my training days and my competitions. I would target particular competitions that I wanted to win, while setting others as preparation events where other factors were the goals for the particular event. When I started playing more regularly in bridge competitions, I applied the same approach to bridge as I had done in my sporting career and I set myself some specific measurable goals such as:

» finishing in the top ten in every congress pairs event I played for the year;

» achieving over 58% in 90% of club duplicate (matchpoint) sessions;

» learn to play the Acol system in the next three months;

» reduce the percentage of bidding errors I made in a session by 5% over the next three months.

While score-based goals are an assessment of how well you are playing, they do not necessarily provide you with the information you require to improve your overall performance. They are simply an indicator of progress. To gain real improvement one must undertake a systematic analysis of weaknesses in your game together with the development of a plan to address those areas. In other words, comprehensive performance evaluation must take place. It is important to understand that improvement takes time, and results don't always happen overnight.

To undertake performance evaluation, as a first step, identify some specific parameters that you will evaluate to determine both where your errors are occurring, and how you are tracking against those parameters. Analysis of specific metrics (e.g. defensive errors, lead errors, play errors, bidding errors, etc.) and tracking your performance against those metrics can help you to understand your current weaknesses and target your practice towards improving in those areas.

This record-keeping will also help you determine whether you need to make changes to your system (e.g. not reaching the right contract) or whether you simply need to improve your skills as a player (not making the required number of tricks or not defeating contracts). Metrics also help you make informed decisions on your performance, rather than deciding something is or isn't working based on a feeling, or worse, blaming your partner for your results.

Every elite athlete periodically goes through a detailed evaluation of their performance in competition and training. This evaluation considers a few factors such as:

> » Are my goals being met?

> » Is my competition plan effective?

> » Do I have any technical flaws or areas which are not as consistent as they should be?

> » What can I change to help me achieve my goals?

Keeping a record of your performance and results is extremely important in order to enable you to undertake a data-based analysis of your results.

Sample analysis—Fantunes[1]

A leading Australian player, Bill Jacobs, wrote an article a few years ago where he detailed his analysis of his own partnership's use of the Fantunes

---

[1]   Fantunes is the name of the bridge bidding system used by Italian born tournament players Claudio Nunes and Fulvio Fantoni. The Fantunes system differs in approach from other bidding systems used by world class bridge players. Opening bids of one and two of a suit are stronger than in most systems, with one level suit openings natural and forcing for one round. The one no-trump opening denotes a balanced or semi-balanced hand with 12-14 HCP which can include a singleton or a 5-card major suit. Two-level opening bids are constructive.
Bill Jacobs has also written a book on the system entitled Fantunes Revealed which won the International Bridge Press Association Book of the Year prize for 2013.
Claudio Nunes and Fulvio Fantoni were found guilty of cheating in 2015 and received various bans from different federations. Refer https://en.wikipedia.org/wiki/Fantoni_and_Nunes_cheating_scandal

system and how he had compared the results the partnership achieved using the Fantunes system with the results they might have achieved using their traditional bidding methods for a two-year period.

In this analysis, Jacobs evaluated 1,459 hands where he and his partner opened the bidding at the one or two level. For each hand he compared the result they achieved using Fantunes compared with the result they would have hypothetically achieved had they been playing Standard American and converted this result to a positive or negative imp score. This data was collated in a spreadsheet and totalled to produce a summary of data, which showed whether the new system gave better results than their old methods. A summary of the results of the data analysis is shown below:

Fantunes opening	# deals	Average IMPs per deal for Fantunes
1C	300	-0.9
1D	123	+1.4
1H/1S	282	+0.3
1NT	398	+0.7
2C/D/H/S	313	+2.5
Pass*	43	-5.3
Total	1459	+0.5

* Deals which would have been opened a weak two in Standard American.

An evaluation like the one Jacobs conducted will give a partnership confidence that the change which has been made to the partnership methods is superior. It removes the doubts that arise when a partnership has a poor board, and 'thinks' they would have had a better result using the partnership's old methods. Certainly, on a specific board this may hold true. However to achieve success in bridge, we want to use methods which will give good results on the highest percentage of boards in the long run.

Analysing performance – a basic methodology

In training for shooting competitions, I used to record everything I tried. I would then assess all changes for their effectiveness using detailed performance analysis. I feel it is equally important to do this for bridge. As an example, keeping a record of your competition results is great with respect to determining whether you are getting better results as a player, but not very helpful in analysing performance.

A more useful analysis would be to set up a spreadsheet[2], or simply a page of graph paper with the following headings (you can add more, but this is a good starting point).

- » B - Bidding error (for example did you make the right bid in accordance with your system agreement);

- » J - Judgement error (for example over-valued/under-valued your hand and overbid/underbid);

- » DP - Declarer play error;

- » D - Defensive error;

- » L - Poor lead;

- » C - Concentration error; (e.g. revoke, bid out of turn, etc.).

- » S - System error (where your system prevented you getting to the right contract)

Once you have your spreadsheet set up, you need to do some data gathering over a period of time. One day's play will not provide enough data to make an informed decision, as you may only get one or two examples in a session with obvious boards which fall into the above categories. You need at least 300 boards or more to have enough data to start to conduct meaningful analysis.

---

2   Appendix 4: Sample Spreadsheet Analysis

Go through every hand you play in competition and classify the hands where your score was below par or where you can identify that you could have done better, based on what everyone else in the event did. Be careful not to measure yourself against double dummy analysis like Deep Finesse—this is the optimal result if you could see everyone's cards and is often unrealistic at the table.

» Get your partner to do the same assessment on the same boards independently and compare notes.

» Be as objective as you possibly can. Unless you are quite advanced players, don't worry too much if you cannot categorise the marginal hands—they probably aren't the ones costing you results. If a decision is very close, that means that the difference that your decision makes will be small in the long run. Be more focussed on the glaring errors.

» Eliminate hands where you have a choice of lines of play such as whether to finesse one way or the other—even top players may choose the wrong way in these circumstances.

When you identify the area(s) in which you make the most errors, you can analyse that area in more detail and then develop a plan to improve in that area. For example, you might find you frequently fail in contracts where you are declarer in 3NT. Or you may find that you allow contracts that should be defeated to make or give away too many overtricks and you need to sharpen your defence. Or you may find you make the wrong choices on when and when not to sacrifice over the opponent's game. Or you may find you aren't bidding the 'good' slams.

Develop a plan for how you will improve that aspect. You might read some books on the topic, or do some specific practice in the area. Work on it until you no longer have that as a problem and then move on to the next area you identify for improvement. Over time you will reduce your errors. You will know your plan is working because you will have the data to support your analysis. You will also find you are getting closer to achieving your goals.

If you aren't too serious and just like to play socially, then I expect this is going to be more effort than you want to put into your game. Gaining incremental improvement takes time and diligent application once the basics are understood and learned. However, it is far better to use an analytical methodology like this than relying on perception or gut feel. Like champion sportspeople, the bridge players who are the most successful are not only those who make the fewest errors or who have the most talent, but those who also work the hardest at improving their game.

As you become more advanced you will be able to further define categories, and identify and classify smaller errors, and be more analytical of your performance, but in the beginning working on the obvious mistakes will make a huge difference to your game.

Using this methodology, my partner made a change to our system to better deal with hands where our side showed a strong 2NT opening. We decided that after a transfer bid, accepting the transfer showed three-card support, bidding four of the major showed four card support and 3NT would show no support. We then developed a number of continuations to help us improve our slam bidding. We got to test our new methods on this deal:

Dealer: East

Vulnerable: EW

```
                      ♠ K1076532
                      ♥ A9
                      ♦ -
                      ♣ Q863
        ♠ J                        ♠ 84
        ♥ 754                      ♥ K63
        ♦ J10964                   ♦ Q8532
        ♣ 9754                     ♣ AJ2
                      ♠ AQ9
                      ♥ QJ1082
                      ♦ AK7
                      ♣ K10
```

West	North	East	South
		Pass	2NT
Pass	3♥[1]	Pass	3♠[2]
Pass	4♦[3]	Pass	4♠[4]
Pass	4NT[4]	Pass	5♣[6]
Pass	6♠	All Pass	

1 - Transfer to spades

2 - Three-card support for spades

3 - Voidwood, asking for keycards outside diamonds

4 - One or four keycards

5 - Asking for the queen of trumps

6 - Yes and the king of clubs

On the lead of the jack of diamonds, it is a simple matter to pitch a heart and club and give up the ace of clubs to make twelve tricks.

While most might reach the slam using normal methods, it is a great confidence boost to know your methods allowed you to find out your partner's exact holding so that you could bid the slam with confidence knowing that you didn't have two quick club losers.

Evaluating what works in your game

So far in this chapter I have discussed using data analysis to help identify and address areas of weakness. Another important use of data analysis is to identify what is working.

Achieving improvement in the early stages of your bridge career, as in all types of competition, is relatively straightforward. It is easy to make progress when there are a lot of areas that need improvement and you will find that progress is rapid. It gets much harder when you become a more experienced player and you have achieved a reasonable level of competence. Now improvement comes more slowly and is focussed on three primary areas:

» continued development of your skill as a player;

» incremental improvements to your system with your partner; and,

» development of your partnership harmony and understanding.

This correlation between improvement and time is shown in the graphic on the next page.

Elite athletes adopt a very structured and systematic approach to changing the technical aspects of their game and even to changes in how they are training. For example, an athlete may decide that they have maximised their performance level using a particular technical skill, or indeed that they need to begin using a more advanced skill in competition as their existing arsenal of skills will not score enough points in competition. A diver might be able to execute a double somersault perfectly and while this may be sufficient for them to win in junior ranks, that degree of difficulty in open competition is not high enough to score the points needed to win. A new skill must be added such as a triple somersault, which will score more points.

Similarly, in bridge, using simple Blackwood or Gerber to ask for Aces may be sufficient in club competition, but in state or national level competition,

Technical Excerpt

Stages of Skill Acquisition Continuum[1]

There are three stages of skill acquisition that sit along a continuum of skill learning. The cognitive stage is characterised by frequent errors and is the stage when the learner has to think a lot about the skill and how to execute it. They also require lots of frequent feedback and help from an instructor.

The associative stage is the largest and longest stage. It is characterised by lots of practice. As the player progresses towards the next stage, errors become less frequent and smaller.

The final stage is the autonomous stage. This stage is characterised by few errors and those which do occur are minor. A player at this stage of skill acquisition can think about other aspects of competition and not think at all about the skill itself.

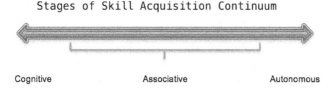

Stages of Skill Acquisition Continuum

Cognitive   Associative   Autonomous

The above is true for developing and changing your system, although the learning curve is generally faster because of the acquired knowledge already present.

---

1   Adapted from: https://www.pdhpe.net/factors-affecting-performance/how-does-the-acquisition-of-skill-affect-performance/stages-of-skill-acquisition/

a more sophisticated method such as combining cue-bidding and Roman Keycard Blackwood will be required. Or you may find you are good at playing hands very quickly and that this works well at the local bridge club, but when you try this approach at national congress level, your results go down. You might need to add another skill to your toolbox (slower, technical play) in order to achieve your goals.

When athletes implement change to any technical skill it is extremely well planned. Key characteristics of the change are:

» the change happens in the off season;

» hours of practice are expended to learn the change before it is used in an important competition; and,

» there is reasonable confidence that a change is required to achieve improvement—i.e. the current technique is not going to deliver the necessary results at the next level.

The reason for this highly structured approach to changes is that it is important an athlete heads into competition feeling confident that their technical skills are robust and will withstand the pressure of competition. This mental confidence in your skills is vital as any doubts in the mind will translate into fear in execution and an increased likelihood of mistakes.

Similarly, in bridge, analysis of your existing system and skill level is necessary before you decide to make any changes. Consider this deal:

Dealer: North

Vulnerable: All

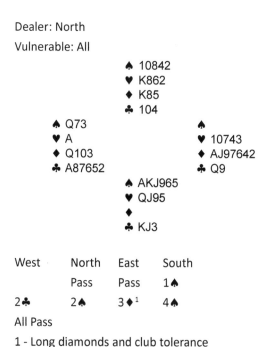

West	North	East	South
	Pass	Pass	1♠
2♣	2♠	3♦¹	4♠

All Pass

1 - Long diamonds and club tolerance

Here East-West (both international players) missed the opportunity to bid five diamonds which makes on careful play.

This pair may have had an agreement to avoid pre-empting in second seat when holding a four-card major as a side suit, an approach which many pairs adopt. Or East may simply have been reluctant to pre-empt in second seat. Hence, the question to decide before making any change to your system agreements is: was the approach a failing with the system, or was there a failing in judgement?

If a failing in system then some further analysis could be undertaken by the pair. System failures can be assessed by considering how many times similar issues cause you to miss a game or sacrifice, as well as how many other pairs who did not have this agreement found their way to five diamonds. Did this pair's agreement make it too difficult to find the right contract? Was this board an isolated instance? On balance does the agreement work for the pair more frequently than not?

Despite the initial pass, the player sitting East later told me when asked about the hand that he could have taken an action over four spades such as four no-trumps which would have indicated two places to play, and West could now have bid five diamonds. This would have placed the North-South pair in a predicament as to whether to try five spades.

Should a pair who have this type of agreement decide that they wanted to reconsider their approach, collecting data on similar hands and the plus and minus results for the pair would assist in making an informed decision about changing the system agreement.

A key question for the bridge player to examine is whether the weaker performance is due to an error in judgement or a deficiency in skill or a sub-optimal system or method. Just as tennis players often choose a highly risky shot at the wrong point in a match rather than waiting for the correct moment, bridge players will often bid for a wildly optimistic game or slam when a part score or game is enough.

If this is happening with you and your partner, then changing your methods or conventions might not enable the performance improvement you are seeking. Similarly, if your deficiencies are due to a lack of knowledge of card play techniques such as squeezes, finesses, card combinations or percentage plays, then work in this area might be prudent before system changes are made.

Think carefully about whether you want to be making a change when your partner says something like "I heard about this great convention that we should use. It doesn't come up very often, maybe once a year, but it is really good and it will help us a lot". Yikes—all that effort to learn an obscure convention that comes up once a year may not be the best plan!

However, if after analysis you decide that a change to your current methods is necessary, then I believe that, like elite sportspeople, you need to follow a structured process to implement that change. As an example, you could take all the hand records from events in which you have played in the last six months and gather your results. With computer and web-based scoring, and the ready availability of hand records after every session, this information is available, if somewhat time-consuming to put together. You can then use this data for some of the analysis described below.

If you are going to pursue this then firstly, identify the 'one' convention or method you want to change. Let's say you decide that using Bergen[3] raises after a major suit opening might be better than using your current method of mini-splinters (where 1S - 3C shows four-card spade support, short clubs and invitational values, etc.).

» Identify from your collected data every hand where you used or would have used a mini-splinter.

» Evaluate the result you got on each board in terms of plus or minus IMPs compared to both par and the field in the event. (Note: sometimes it is not possible to get to the par contract.)

» Now go through all the hands again and assess what result bidding those hands using Bergen raises would have provided. Include hands where a Bergen raise applies even if a mini-splinter does not apply.

» Assess whether the new method will give you an average net imp gain or not.

» Assess whether you will be able to use the new convention more frequently than the old convention.

The question you are trying to answer is: "will this change give me a better performance level?". It is easy to say—"Can't I just ask good players what they think?" Well, of course you can do that, and you probably should ask

---

3   Bergen raises (invented by Marty Bergen) use a bid of three clubs to show four-card support for the major suit opener and 6 - 9 points or four diamonds to show four-card support and 10 - 12 points. A jump in the other major shows three card support and 10 - 12 points. An immediate jump to three major is a pre-emptive raise showing 0 - 5 points. Bergen raises are often combined with Jacoby 2NT.
        Many players now reverse the meaning of three clubs and three diamonds and some elect not to use the bid of the other major to show the three card raise at all.

their opinion. But taking the time to do the analysis yourself will reinforce your belief that the change will work and that the decision is correct.

You might decide to make the change. After using your new convention, you should do further analysis to see if the change makes you and your partner stronger or weaker as a pair. Did it work as you expected it would from your analysis? You can do this by assessing your results on the hands where the method or convention applied, compared with the result you would expect to have achieved using a natural method and/or your old convention.

Analysis of hands is relatively easy to perform, provided that you are willing to spend the time. Using a data-based approach when making changes to your system or play rather than making changes based upon gut feel or instinct will give you the confidence to believe in yourself when using those changes in competition.

Like any activity, data analysis becomes easier the more you do it, so even if it takes time initially, you will find you will become quicker at analysis the more you do it.

To some, this might all seem like a lot of work but gaining incremental improvement is hard once the basics are understood and learned. The reason people become champions in their chosen activity is not only because they have some ability, but because they work hard at their game.

Developing partnership harmony and understanding

When I originally wrote about this concept in a shorter article for a magazine, I shared my article with David Morgan[4] who rightly identified the third aspect mentioned earlier—building partnership understanding and harmony. This is one of my personal improvement goals, so I am going to use David's comments to begin expanding on this point:

---

4   David Morgan was Australian Open Team Captain in 2014.

"Working to get the best out of each other is an important goal for any serious partnership to have. There may be some people who respond well to being criticised after a hand, but I don't think I've ever seen that happen at the table. Beyond working out when and how to discuss what happens when things go wrong, it's worthwhile to work on helping partner to play better.

Maybe partner likes to be complimented after doing something well, even if it is routine; if so, compliment them.

Maybe partner plays better when there's little discussion; save the chat for after play finishes.

Maybe partner likes a smile to reassure them after they've made a mistake; smile.

Maybe partner likes the suits laid out in a particular way when you're dummy; do it!

Maybe partner really doesn't like it when you leave the table when you're dummy except in an emergency; respect their wishes."

Building a great partnership doesn't happen overnight. While it is true that one player might be the senior or more experienced partner of the pair, each must treat the other as an equal and respect the other's game and abilities. Here are some of the factors that a few of the great sporting partnerships have highlighted as reasons for their success:

Jayne Torvill and Christopher Dean, the ice-dancing Olympic champion pair, attributed single-mindedness, friendship, attention to detail, similar mindsets and similar work ethic as key factors in their success.

Mark Woodbridge (half of the champion tennis doubles pair of Woodford & Woodbridge) was reported as saying communication was key. He said "Anytime Mark and I held something in and didn't let each other know how we felt, we never played well together. We knew what we were doing was like a business and we had to be professional. We had our moments when we hacked each other off and would have liked to have gone another way.

But we realised we had something that was too good."[5]

Bridge champions Eric Rodwell and Jeff Meckstroth have often engendered a feeling of dread in their opponents. Opponents feel they need to take big risks simply to compete on level terms. Here is a hand from the 2008 Spingold Tournament which illustrates why:[6]

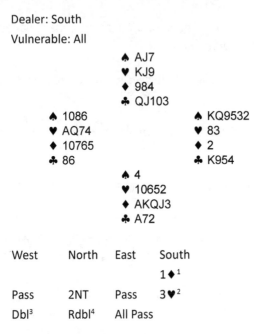

Dealer: South
Vulnerable: All

```
                          ♠ AJ7
                          ♥ KJ9
                          ♦ 984
                          ♣ QJ103
         ♠ 1086                         ♠ KQ9532
         ♥ AQ74                         ♥ 83
         ♦ 10765                        ♦ 2
         ♣ 86                           ♣ K954
                          ♠ 4
                          ♥ 10652
                          ♦ AKQJ3
                          ♣ A72
```

West	North	East	South
			1♦[1]
Pass	2NT	Pass	3♥[2]
Dbl[3]	Rdbl[4]	All Pass	

1 - Either diamonds or a weak no-trump

2 - Values for game, shortage in spades

3 - Lead directing double against a possible 3NT contract

4 - If you are happy to play here partner, so am I

Against three hearts redoubled, West led the eight of clubs.

Meckstroth played the queen of clubs from dummy, which held the trick, then ran the jack of clubs which also held. He next led a diamond to his ace

5   ESPN interview
6   First published: The Guardian. 28 July 2008

and a heart up, playing the jack when West played low. Another diamond was led from dummy, which East could have ruffed – but the defender had to hope that his partner would have something good in diamonds, so he discarded a spade. Winning with the king, Meckstroth played another heart, dummy's nine holding the trick when West again ducked.

If you think that West was now bound to make two trump tricks, holding the ace and queen of hearts against North's singleton king, you haven't seen Meckstroth the magician at work. He played two more rounds of diamonds, discarding a club from the table, then led a spade to the ace and ruffed a spade. When he played his fifth diamond, West could do nothing, and Meckstroth emerged with twelve tricks and a score of 1360, losing just the ace of trumps.

Here, confidence in their system agreements, combined with trust in partner's bidding allowed this champion pair to achieve a huge score on what should otherwise have been a flat board.

As I have stated previously, the players who are the most successful, are not just those who make the fewest errors, but those who also work the hardest at improving their game. Most importantly, the best competitors are those who believe in their own ability and techniques, even if they are not quite perfect. Most of all though, they believe in and trust their partner.

Working on improving your game may also be assisted by developing an Annual Training Plan. I have outlined a basic method for developing this in Appendix 2.

Chapter 9

Match Pressure

"In a sportsperson's life, pressure is always there. You have to learn to deal with it."

- Mary Kom, world amateur boxing champion

Pressure comes in varying forms in any type of competition. Whether it is the pressure of expectations, time pressure to finish because you are a slow player or have slow opponents or simply the pressure you put on yourself to perform, pressure also exists in bridge. All of us have felt pressure in some activity we have undertaken at some time in our lives.

Think about how many times you have made a basic error and thought afterwards "how could I possibly have done that?". At those times it might simply have been you were feeling the pressure of the situation.

This next deal where North-South reached the grand slam in spades illustrates how pressure can have an impact on our thinking.

Dealer: East

Vulnerable: All

```
                    ♠ 98753
                    ♥
                    ♦ AJ1096
                    ♣ AK6
        ♠ 102                   ♠ Q
        ♥ K932                  ♥ 10864
        ♦ 52                    ♦ Q8743
        ♣ Q10943               ♣ 752
                    ♠ AKJ64
                    ♥ AQJ75
                    ♦ K
                    ♣ J8
```

On the lead of the ten of spades, thirteen tricks can be claimed by drawing two rounds of trumps, pitching dummy's losing club on the ace of hearts (or declarer's fourth losing heart on dummy's ace of diamonds); cashing the king of diamonds, and ruffing dummy's three losing diamonds (or declarer's three remaining losing hearts). I was declarer in the above hand and my partner and I were leading the event at the time which brings its own kind of pressure. Consequently, I couldn't see this obvious line immediately. I had to slow down and take my time to ensure I took the correct line to make the contract. A hand that would normally have been routine for me was made much more difficult by the pressure involved in the situation. Although I eventually made the contract, it is easy to imagine myself making some mistake - and pressure would have undoubtedly been to blame.

There are various factors which go to increasing the pressure felt here in addition to leading the event. Since bidding and playing a grand slam is an infrequent occurrence there is already a little bit of an unfamiliar environment which can heighten one's anxiety level. As there are a lot of IMPs at stake, the 'fear of failure' can increase the pressure felt. Finally, as everyone knows success or failure in a slam or grand slam will frequently determine the outcome in the match, thereby adding to the overall pressure of the situation.

Why do we feel pressure or anxiety in competition?

There is a saying that the young have no fear. Certainly, this was true for me in the early stages of my shooting career. I used to love knowing what score I needed to win the event going into the last round. Often it was unavoidable because other shooters would come up to me and tell me! Nothing like a bit of gamesmanship to try and throw you off your game. My response more often than not was to get that score. I was lucky enough to be able to ignore the comments and perform at my best. When you are young or newer to an activity you don't really have a comfort zone since you don't have a record to defend, you have fewer preconceived ideas, and you have fewer 'skeletons in the closet' or 'unfinished business', a phrase that often gets used by sporting commentators. There is less likely to be the 'weight of expectations' on your shoulders. As we compete more and are more successful, we start to enter events with a pre-conceived idea of how we might perform and the match pressure is greater.

In shooting finals each competitor's level of anxiety was already high, which is natural when competing in a final of an event. Adding to this anxiety was time pressure. Since each shot had a short time limit, pressure came from the scorer calling out the result for each shot and the competitor's placing after every one of the ten shots in the final[1], and the cheers or groans of the spectators depending on how their 'favourite' was performing. All of this added to the pressure the athlete felt.

One disastrous example of pressure, which I witnessed, occurred when a shooter in the final of the Olympic event shot on the wrong target, scoring a zero and losing the gold medal in the process. The same shooter made a remarkable recovery from this disappointment to go on and win the gold medal in his next event, but losing the gold in such a way must have been quite devastating. To recover from that disappointment to go on and win his next event showed remarkable resilience. Incredibly four years later the same shooter was in another final and did a similar thing,

---

[1]   Note that the format for shooting finals has been changed since my competitive days and some of these comments regarding the format are not applicable now.

missing the target altogether when he accidentally touched his trigger and fired too early! The Olympics are widely considered to be the biggest pressure cooker in sport and many athletes stumble on the biggest stage due to match pressure. I heard this shooter talk about what happened afterwards and he said that it sometimes happened because of the setup with his rifle, but it would also be easy to attribute this shooter's error to match pressure.

Similarly, in bridge events, a player who consistently finishes in the top ten might start the event feeling like they should finish around where they normally do. This can inadvertently create some pressure to perform. For some the weight of expectations can be detrimental and result in increased nervousness, loss of concentration and errors. Yerkes-Dodson's Law shows the arousal curve (refer page 20). From this curve we see that a little bit of pressure is good since a slightly increased arousal level heightens awareness and can actually improve performance. However, when the pressure tips the player over into an anxious state, performance suffers. Studies have shown that when a competitor has reached this overly anxious state, they will often make errors they would not normally make, since their ability to process data is inhibited[2].

Of course, the level of a competition will also change the level of pressure or anxiety a player feels. There is a significant difference between playing in an international or national event and playing at your local club. We also know from the discussion on comfort zones (Chapter 5) that the pressure a player feels can change depending on the performance level and also whom they are playing. When outside their comfort zone, competitors can make errors when performing in competition because they become anxious or nervous due to their performance exceeding their expectations or because of the environment in which they find themselves.

On this deal from a tournament we played the pair who were leading in the third round out of eight. As my partner (West) thought we were behind at this point in the match, she pushed hard to get us to slam in

---

2   Several research articles are available on this topic. Most specifically by Moser et al.

hearts. In reality we were actually ahead at this point in the match, but perceptions during a match can often be misleading.

Here's what happened:

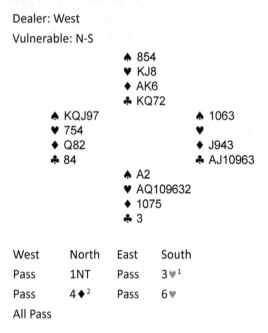

Dealer: West
Vulnerable: N-S

```
                    ♠ 854
                    ♥ KJ8
                    ♦ AK6
                    ♣ KQ72
    ♠ KQJ97                      ♠ 1063
    ♥ 754                        ♥
    ♦ Q82                        ♦ J943
    ♣ 84                         ♣ AJ10963
                    ♠ A2
                    ♥ AQ109632
                    ♦ 1075
                    ♣ 3
```

West	North	East	South
Pass	1NT	Pass	3♥[1]
Pass	4♦[2]	Pass	6♥
All Pass			

1 - Natural slam try asking about range and keycards
2 - Two keycards, no Q♥, better than minimum opening

On the lead of the king of spades, the slam is doomed to fail. All East needs to do is hold on to the ace of clubs and a spade. What happened at the table on the run of all the hearts but one, was that East needed to find six discards. Perhaps he didn't have a good picture of declarer's hand or maybe he lost concentration and didn't pay enough attention to his partner's discards and count the hand out properly. Perhaps East had placed declarer with a singleton spade and four diamonds (or perhaps even five diamonds and a club void?). For whatever reason he misjudged the defence completely and threw two spades and four clubs which left this end position:

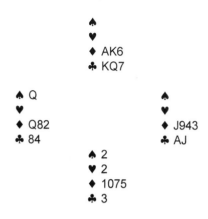

```
              ♠
              ♥
              ♦ AK6
              ♣ KQ7
  ♠ Q                    ♠
  ♥                      ♥
  ♦ Q82                  ♦ J943
  ♣ 84                   ♣ AJ
              ♠ 2
              ♥ 2
              ♦ 1075
              ♣ 3
```

Failing to keep parity with dummy's clubs (and failing to keep a spade) was a fatal mistake which allowed the contract to make when the seven of clubs became high for declarer's twelfth trick.

This was an uncharacteristic error from a good quality pair. Keeping diamonds was irrational—if declarer had diamond length they could always have ruffed any losers in the dummy, so partner must be placed with the queen.

What causes a good player in a leading position in a competition to make this type of error? Is it the pressure from being in a leading position that causes the player to make an error which at other times wouldn't occur? Is it some other distraction that happened earlier in the day that meant the player wasn't concentrating sufficiently? Sometimes it might be a combination of factors. The point here is that when you find yourself in a winning position, the increased pressure can cause errors which might otherwise not occur. It is likely that if this hand had been played in the first match of the day, before any pressure had materialised, North-South would have played in 4♥ and East-West would have taken two tricks on defence rather than one.

While it's true that knowing approximately where you are running is unavoidable—after all if you are at table one in a Swiss movement, you know you are probably coming first or second—there is no reason to exacerbate the problem. Some players enhance this anxiety by spending a lot of time looking at the scoreboard between rounds. This is guaranteed to make you start thinking about the outcome (winning/losing), rather than the task at hand—making or defending this contract, bidding according to your system, and so on.

Some players have no problem with knowing how they are performing, and some even thrive on it, lifting their performance when they have a chance to win. However, if you are not one of those (rare) players, and your history is that you choke or make mistakes when the pressure is on, then finding a way to deal with this anxiety is just as important as working on your bidding, card play and defence.

Avoiding looking at your score is one tactic which can be tried. This was employed by the winning Ashton team at the 2019 Autumn Nationals in Australia. They chose to not score up during the final and three of the four team members didn't know the margin until the end. (The most experienced team member, Sartaj Hans, kept track of things to make sure there were no scoring errors). Employing this one simple tactic worked for them! Another tactic is to segment your performance and set segment goals.

Segmenting performance and segment goals

Segmenting performance makes a player focus on achievable goals rather than the overall outcome. In shooting my match could be broken into parts and it was quite easy for me to set segment goals. For example, a match was 60 shots, so it was broken into 5 or 10 shot segments with a goal for each segment which concentrated on technical factors rather than scores. This had the effect of focussing my mind on my technique rather than the score. In tennis a segment could be each game or set. The player might focus on some basic technical fundamentals like follow through or watching the ball on to the racquet. The theory here is that by focussing on process or technique you forget about the result or how well you are doing. This change in how you focus your thoughts can create less anxiety or stress and lead to a better outcome.

How could this type of methodology translate into application at the bridge table?

Most of our bridge competitions are made up of multiple segments. For example:

» A one-day Swiss pairs or teams' event might be 7 x 8 board matches or similar – each match is a segment.

» A competition at your club might be made up of 2 x 14 board rounds per day or night over a number of weeks – each round could be a segment.

» A duplicate game consists of 2, 3 or 4 boards against each pair of opponents – each pair of opponents could be treated as a segment.

While the overall goal is to win the day/event and ideally you would like to win each match or round, setting sub-goals for each segment and achieving these sub-goals can assist with helping you forget about the game you just went off in or the slam you missed and get you thinking more about getting the process right. Focussing your thoughts on process is more likely to lead to a good overall performance. Often the bad result isn't so bad anyway—everyone else might have had the same result and you have simply given yourself a big negative chip on your shoulder by imagining it was bad, or that you are not doing well in the round. Having a way of letting the negative results be bygones lets you focus on getting the job done on the next deal.

In duplicate pairs many players might set a score-based goal as simple as getting a plus score on every board. Even if the opponents have the cards their way, a 'plus' could still be to ensure the overtricks are kept to a minimum or even defeating a contract through careful defence or subterfuge by making an unexpected lead or play. Endeavouring to play consistent bridge is always the objective. However, generally segment goals comprise a combination of factors which may include this score goal and additionally some technique goal(s), a personal improvement goal, and so on. Hence the segment goals for duplicate pairs could become:

» Get a 'plus' score on every board; and/or

» Count the hand out before playing to trick one; and/or

» No chatting about the hand after the play; and/or.......

Segment goals can be further defined. For example, let's consider the segment goal 'counting the hand before playing to trick one', and how this might apply depending upon your level of skill and expertise:

» **For a basic level player** as declarer in a contract, this could mean thinking about the opening lead before you play to trick one and trying to count that suit before playing. Think about what is in the leader's hand, what is in your hand, what is in dummy, what is in the fourth player's hand. You have a lot of information from the bidding or from the card that is led. You can often get a good picture of the distribution in a suit by undertaking this simple exercise.

» **For an intermediate player**, counting can advance to considering the shape of the whole hand of your partner or the opponent, based on the lead, what you can see of dummy and the bidding.

» **For a more advanced player**, this thinking could consider what inferences can be drawn from this lead, as opposed to some other lead that might have been made. Throughout the hand continuing to consider what card is played, and by deduction what this implies, continues the focus on this segment goal.

Occupying the mind with a technical aspect like counting the hand decreases the likelihood that anxiety created by thoughts about scores and winning/losing will have an effect on performance during the match. Eventually this approach to each hand becomes automatic and the segment goals can be redefined to other areas for focus. Throughout the day, a different goal can be used in each segment so that the player's focus remains sharp. Players should set goals that help their particular performance objectives.

The best players know when a contract should or shouldn't have been made immediately after the hand, but less experienced players don't always know this until they see the hand record or the result. There is a temptation to become distracted by the thought that a contract should have been bid or made, or a particular defence employed—whether or not it is true.

It is also easy to get distracted in a segment of the match by the perception that the cards aren't running your way and no matter what you do, you have no chance. Staying away from the scoreboard and thoughts about your placing or winning and keeping your mind on segment goals can improve concentration and performance to ensure your results are the best they can be.

At a recent Swiss Pairs' tournament my partner and I were in contention to win going into the last round when this hand hit the table as the third board in the set:

Dealer: East
Vulnerable: E-W

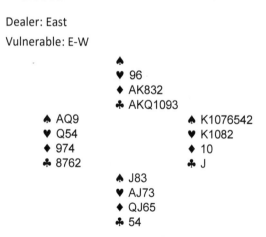

Over partner's pre-emptive three spades the auction was passed around to North who bashed six clubs. On the lead of the ten of diamonds, declarer drew trumps and claimed. It was pretty clear this was going to be a poor board for us as many pairs in the Swiss event[3] will not have the methods to allow them to reach slam on the board. In fact, this pair didn't really have a method either—they just took a punt at it.

Rather than dwelling on what had happened and whether this was a good or bad outcome for our side (it was very bad and everyone at the table knew it) we just moved on to the next board which turned the match back our way:

Dealer: South
Vulnerable: All

```
                        ♠ Q5432
                        ♥ 104
                        ♦ 73
                        ♣ J532
        ♠ KJ9                           ♠ 1086
        ♥ 632                           ♥ AKQ985
        ♦ KQ942                         ♦ A5
        ♣ Q7                            ♣ A4
                        ♠ A7
                        ♥ J7
                        ♦ J1086
                        ♣ K10986
```

West	North	East	South
			Pass
1♦[1]	Pass	1♥	Pass
2♥	Pass	4NT[2]	Pass
5♣[3]	Pass	6♥	All Pass

1 - Five or more diamonds

2 - Roman keycard blackwood

3 - zero or three keycards

---

3   Note that 7♦ makes on the board. While expert players might have the methods to reach this contract, players in a state or county level event such as the one we were contesting are less likely to possess the necessary skills and techniques.

After the lead of the ace of spades and a spade won by dummy's king, with limited entries to the West hand, I tested hearts which I was happy to see break 2-2. As long as diamonds broke no worse than 4-2, I had twelve tricks now, with the six of hearts providing a late entry to the established diamonds.

This board provided a huge contribution to our score and assisted us with a win in the event. I saw the opponents literally slump in their seats after it. Even though both sides had successfully bid a slam, the approach following each result was very different—we tried not to let their good score distract us, while our making slam had an obvious effect on the opponents and contributed to their lack of success in the crucial final round.

Staying focussed and keeping your attention on the next board rather than focussing on what has occurred previously in the round or the feeling that the cards are running against you is important to achieving success in competition.

Time pressure

Another type of pressure experienced in matches is brought about by the time limits for the round. A key contributor which can increase match anxiety is when play is slow and the time limit for the match is approaching the end. I am sure we have all been at tables where players rush to try and finish so as to complete all of the boards for the set. After all, you paid your money for a certain number of boards, so you absolutely have to finish, don't you? Often this haste will create a very bad result on one board because the players don't take their 'normal' amount of time to bid or play and a silly error occurs as a result.

Let's consider what the outcomes might be if a board is missed:

- **The flat board**: If the contract available is a game that everyone will bid and make, then if you miss this board there is no real problem as both pairs will get an average score (assuming that your side isn't penalised by the director).

- **The swing board in your favour**: If your methods would have enabled you to reach a good contract compared with the opponents/rest of the field, then you have missed a chance to swing the round your way, and you are going to be pretty annoyed if you miss this board and it costs you a place.

- **The swing board against you**: If it is a board that your opponents might have got a good result in their favour then you will probably be quite happy to have missed it.

- **The board your team-mates did well on**: These are the real nightmares. The opponents had a bidding mix-up and your team-mates scored +1100. You missed this board due to slow play—ouch! Now you might also have grumpy team-mates.

On this board played in the penultimate round of a major national pairs event, my partner and I benefitted from running out of time in the round when we didn't get to play the final board. On this occasion, there had been some tricky boards requiring a lot of thought by both sides and we just didn't get to play this board. Since both sides were slow no penalty was applied to either pair[4].

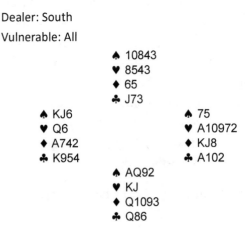

Dealer: South
Vulnerable: All

                    ♠ 10843
                    ♥ 8543
                    ♦ 65
                    ♣ J73
    ♠ KJ6   ♠ 75
    ♥ Q6   ♥ A10972
    ♦ A742   ♦ KJ8
    ♣ K954   ♣ A102
                    ♠ AQ92
                    ♥ KJ
                    ♦ Q1093
                    ♣ Q86

---

4   Note that in some jurisdictions a penalty will automatically be applied to both pairs for slow play.

On their combined 26 points, our opponents sitting East-West would almost certainly have reached game in no-trumps making (on the lie of the cards ten tricks can be made by East-West), so an average on the board was a positive outcome for our side.

It is possible we could have played this board if both pairs had tried to play as fast as possible on the previous two boards when we realised that time was becoming short. But for what purpose? Our results would likely have been worse as we would have had less time to consider our decisions and might have slipped up, potentially creating a big loss on one of the boards. And it would have all been to get the last board on the table, only to sit there and pass throughout while the opponents got to a cold game! Much better to play at your normal speed and try to avoid feeling the pressure created by the clock.

Let's look at another example. On this occasion, the players rushed to play this final board of their round. They put the board on the table just as the bell went for the end of the round, but as they were the two leading teams at the time the director allowed them to play it. The players on the leading team subsequently wished he hadn't.

Dealer: East

Vulnerable: N-S

```
                        ♠ 1032
                        ♥ 7
                        ♦ J1093
                        ♣ AQ986
        ♠ 96                          ♠ AKJ874
        ♥ KJ10543                     ♥ 862
        ♦ 86                          ♦ Q
        ♣ J104                        ♣ 532
                        ♠ Q5
                        ♥ AQ9
                        ♦ AK7542
                        ♣ K7
```

East had opened three spades at one table and quite surprisingly was allowed to play there for one off. At the other (slow) table, the auction proceeded:

West	North	East	South
	Pass	2♠	Dbl
3♠	4♣[1]	Pass	4♦
Pass	5♦	All Pass	

1 - Long hesitation

Five diamonds is untouchable, and the loss of eleven IMPs on the board was costly for the team. Naturally East-West appealed to the director over the hesitation but the result was allowed to stand. Imagine if the pair that was out of time had simply decided not to rush to play the last board!

In many sports, failing to finish in time means you lose the match—your score will never be high enough to make up for the missed shot(s). This is not the case in bridge. Often missing one board will be completely inconsequential for both sides (a flat board), while these preceding examples show that sometimes it will be good for your side and sometimes it will be bad.

Of course, in general it is better if you don't reach the point where you are worried about whether you have enough time left. Some players are just slower than others. While it's true that there are some players who are very considered and thoughtful in their play, many are just sloppy in their time management at the table. Note that I am not suggesting that you should rush to play hands so that you finish all your boards. Some hands do take a lot of thought, and there will be times where you just don't get to finish all the boards for a variety of reasons. However, I am suggesting that there are many things you can do to help prevent rushing at the end of a round and making an error because of it. Some of these are really simple to implement:

» **Arrive at the table early:** Often it is the slowest players that are the last ones to sit down at the table after the movement is called. These players are off making a coffee or in the bathroom or chatting or fussing around somewhere. They get to the table, then find they don't have their pen or their spectacles or they left their system card at the last table. They fuss about looking at your system card. Then they decide to have a chat about what defence they will employ against your no-trump openings or some other slightly unfamiliar convention you happen to play.

The clock shows the match has already been running for well over five minutes before they take their cards out of the first board and think about an opening bid. Five minutes might not seem like much, but in an 8-board round it can make quite a difference to the overall match time. This pair who arrived late might be quite quick players, but it turns out their opponents are very methodical, taking time before each bid and card played. Any surprise the table doesn't complete all their boards?

» **Discuss hands after the round:** There are players who insist on discussing hands between boards or who review the results or who have other mannerisms, all of which slow down the play. At a club duplicate, pairs will often look at the scoring unit or traveller to see what other pairs have done for a particular board or to try and figure out what contract they should have been in. All of this might add to some players' enjoyment of the game, but it isn't particularly good bridge etiquette, and it slows down the game enormously—often making it difficult to finish the round. It's all very well if you have 'easy' boards to play, but when you have one of those really difficult hands that take a long time to play, it's nice to have the full time available for you to do this.

» **Manage your table tempo:** Consider when to write the contract down; make the lead before doing 'personal' things like entering the contract on the scoring unit; think about what card you are going to play if declarer plays that suit; keep your attention on the table instead of what is going on elsewhere in the room; claiming when there are only trumps left or if you know your hand is high; etc. All of these things will help speed up the tempo of play at the table (besides being generally good etiquette).

There are also a few positive steps you can take to address the issues where the opponents are causing the hold-up. You can and should call the director if the opponents are excessively slow or arrive late to the table. Often simply drawing formal attention to the problem (by calling the director) will result in your opponents playing at a normal pace from that point onwards. You can also politely ask opponents who post-mortem or review results to discuss/review the hands later at the end of play. Aside from holding up play, the post-mortem at a neighbouring table has been one which is often the cause of damage to your side.

At a recent tournament my partner and I reached the grand slam in spades on a board. However before we played the hand, one of our opponents called the director and said he overheard the next table talking about 'seven spades'. While neither my partner, nor I heard anything, the result on the board was cancelled and both sides received an adjusted score of +3 (a questionable decision itself). As a result, we drew the match instead of winning by 16 assuming we had played the contract correctly.

Missing the opportunity for a big pickup because of a careless comment from an opponent was pretty annoying. Even more annoying was discovering later that the player talking about the hand at the next table was actually talking about the lead of the seven of spades when they wrote down the result on their scoresheet!

Managing the opponents is always trickier than managing your own actions, so make sure:

» you are not engaging in any of the 'time wasting' activities mentioned in this chapter;

» you have a plan for managing match time, and;

» you maintain good table protocols.

Getting through your matches 'in tempo' will ensure you don't get stressed out when time is running low for the round, and assist you with playing all your boards at the desired level. It will also mean you have more time to relax and recover between rounds.

Finally, managing your own time well will often result in the whole table playing at a good tempo – frequently one side playing slowly will slow down the other side as well (they start looking for what the opponents are thinking about, for example).

While I have discussed the need for good time management, one final observation in this area concerns playing difficult hands or those hands where you have made an error early in the play and now need to work hard to recover. Feeling relaxed enough to take your time in these circumstances is an important skill. Anyone who has ever observed top-level bridge players will notice how calm they are when faced with a difficult problem at the table. They will often think for several minutes about the line to take on a difficult hand, yet when the play is underway and the contract obvious, they will make up this time by claiming the remaining tricks.

On this deal from a recent tournament, our opponents reached a fairly routine four-spade contract on the penultimate board of the round. Yet declarer struggled to think clearly on the board and took a long time to determine the correct line after a careless play at trick two. He apologised on several occasions for thinking about the hand and for the amount of time he was taking to play the hand and seemed stressed by the circumstances.

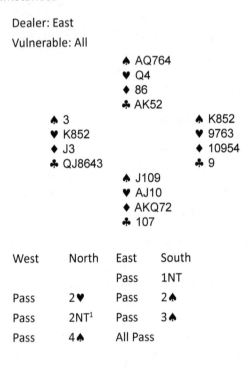

Dealer: East
Vulnerable: All

```
              ♠ AQ764
              ♥ Q4
              ♦ 86
              ♣ AK52
♠ 3                          ♠ K852
♥ K852                       ♥ 9763
♦ J3                         ♦ 10954
♣ QJ8643                     ♣ 9
              ♠ J109
              ♥ AJ10
              ♦ AKQ72
              ♣ 107
```

West	North	East	South
		Pass	1NT
Pass	2♥	Pass	2♠
Pass	2NT[1]	Pass	3♠
Pass	4♠	All Pass	

1 - Artificial, slam interest

Declarer won the queen of clubs lead in dummy and mistakenly continued with the king of clubs. This was ruffed by East, who switched to diamonds. Declarer won in hand and took the losing spade finesse to East who came back a spade. Declarer won in hand and now ran into a mental block on what to do next as West showed out.

He took several minutes to work out the best line to allow him to make his contract after this poor start. Eventually, he worked out the best line was to run two more rounds of diamonds pitching a losing heart from dummy before taking the ruffing finesse in hearts throwing a club: even if East could win, they didn't have any clubs left to play so declarer would be able to draw the last trump and throw dummy's final club on a heart winner.

Note that West could have made declarer's job more difficult by signalling for a heart when North ruffed the king of clubs by following suit with a high club (suit preference). Although the contract can still be made with this continuation it might have increased the pressure on a declarer who had clearly lost focus.

On the board, declarer was perfectly entitled to take his time to think through the best way to make the contract after the early error. His success on the hand was possible because he paused to consider the play (rather than playing fast and trying to finish the match). Since the rest of the match had been played in reasonable tempo there was time to think on this board when declarer faced a mental roadblock on how to play.

Using the tips on the next page to manage the tempo at your table by avoiding actions that waste time will mean you will be well-placed to think carefully when faced with difficult hands or circumstances such as the one this declarer faced.

Tips for time management at the table.

These simple tips will help 'speed up' your play and avoid time pressure in your matches. Most of these are really just normal bridge etiquette anyway:

» Be at the table about five minutes before the scheduled match time to give yourself time to look at the opponent's system card, and discuss any specific defensive methods required with your partner;

» Consider when is the best time to write down the contract and score for the board on your personal scoresheet;

» Make a note on the back of your scoresheet if you want to discuss something about a hand with your partner to remind you to do it after the round, rather than discussing hands during a round/match;

» Have all your required items ready with you (e.g. system card, pen, spectacles, drink);

» Make the director aware mid-way through the round if your opponents are inordinately slow (you may be entitled to compensation if your table doesn't finish, and often the mere fact of drawing attention to the issue will go a long way towards solving it);

» Have a short 'spiel' on your basic system, carding and signalling ready to tell the opponents;

» Claim whenever you can, rather than playing out every card;

» Don't discuss the hand just played in between boards;

» Don't look at the results from boards at other tables in the scoring unit if these results are available to see (you can't change the result, it won't help your play and you can always look up the scores online later).

Chapter 10

Match Fitness

"If you can't outplay them, outwork them."

– Ben Hogan, golfing legend

My partner playing South reached game in hearts on this next deal, which on normal defence is destined to fail.

Dealer: North

Vulnerable: E-W

```
                    ♠ K874
                    ♥ Q1093
                    ♦ K95
                    ♣ Q9
    ♠ A962                      ♠ J103
    ♥ 65                        ♥ J4
    ♦ QJ8                       ♦ 1074
    ♣ AKJ10                     ♣ 87532
                    ♠ Q5
                    ♥ AK872
                    ♦ A632
                    ♣ 64
```

West	North	East	South
	Pass	Pass	1♥
Dbl	2♦[1]	Pass	3♦[2]
Pass	4♥[3]	All pass	

1 - 10+ Heart Raise - may be distribution based

2 - Bid game if you have anything extra

3 - An ambitious evaluation of 'extra'

(Hand repeated below)

```
                    ♠ K874
                    ♥ Q1093
                    ♦ K95
                    ♣ Q9
      ♠ A962                      ♠ J103
      ♥ 65                        ♥ J4
      ♦ QJ8                       ♦ 1074
      ♣ AKJ10                     ♣ 87532
                    ♠ Q5
                    ♥ AK872
                    ♦ A632
                    ♣ 64
```

West got off to a good start by leading the ace-king of clubs, with East giving natural count. Best defence now is to exit a heart and let declarer do all the work, but West chose a different path. He cashed the ace of spades on which East played the jack (promising the ten) before exiting a low spade won in hand by declarer's queen.

Declarer proceeded to play out all the trumps and on the run of the trumps West had to find three pitches. West made a careless error when he failed to keep parity with dummy's spades and chose instead to hold on to diamonds. Declarer could now simply cross to dummy's king of diamonds to throw his two losing diamonds on the king and the now high eight of spades for ten tricks.

This board was played in the second-last round of a one-day event which was held on a hot day in a room with poor air conditioning. Everyone was feeling a bit hot and tired as the day was drawing to a close. The players in question were the second-placed pair in the penultimate round, but this error in defence was a costly one. Had they defended correctly, they would have won the match and gained the leading position going into the last round. In bridge, where tournaments are often quite close, it is these types of errors at critical points which make the difference between winning and losing. Errors like this one are often caused by a loss of concentration, which might be attributed to a lack of match fitness.

What is match fitness?

Many of us may have heard sportspeople talking about being 'match fit'. In bridge, match fitness is about being able to maintain concentration to play throughout a multi-day tournament without becoming overly tired, so that you can play well at the end of a long tournament and not make costly errors like the one which occurred here. Players who have spent most of their time playing at their local club where most of the sessions last about three hours will find their first full day tournament much tougher, while those who enter a multi-day event for the first time will also find they are tiring towards the end of each day, with the final day often being quite a slog. While there is absolutely no question that having a basic level of physical fitness is helpful, even if it is just ensuring you can manage the rigours of travel and long competitions, being 'match fit' has a slightly different connotation.

In sport, coaches often talk about being 'match fit'. Practice form doesn't always translate to the playing field where nerves and the pressure of competition play a part. As an athlete, it doesn't matter how much time you spend on training and practice matches, the first 'real' competition of the season is always hard. It is easy to have a nervous flutter at the beginning of the match or to lose form or focus towards the end of the match. In physical sports, athletes often tire towards the end of the first match of the season, while in mental sports like bridge and chess, it is concentration and focus that suffer. Athletes in all sports and competitions experience this phenomenon of match fitness that shows particularly towards the end of a match, often at the start of the competition season, no matter whether it is football, tennis, chess or bridge. The reasons for this are unclear. It may be the added tension of real competition, the higher level of focus or other factors. However, there is no doubt that the first real competition of the season after a break is substantially harder than playing in practice matches.

Being able to remain focussed and concentrate right through until the last card is played is extremely important and failure to do so can be a sign of a lack of match fitness. Just imagine how disappointed you will feel if you play really well for the first ten boards of a 14-board match, only to find you lose 20 IMPs in the last four boards of the match due to loss of concentration. This is where your match fitness shows.

From the Australian women's team playoffs, the following deal was the penultimate board in the final match of a five-day national tournament, run with several ten-board matches each day. Both pairs at the table were in contention for a place on the national team and both were probably feeling a bit tired and under pressure.

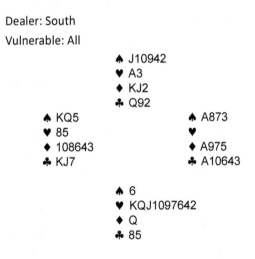

Dealer: South
Vulnerable: All

```
                    ♠ J10942
                    ♥ A3
                    ♦ KJ2
                    ♣ Q92
    ♠ KQ5                       ♠ A873
    ♥ 85                        ♥
    ♦ 108643                    ♦ A975
    ♣ KJ7                       ♣ A10643
                    ♠ 6
                    ♥ KQJ1097642
                    ♦ Q
                    ♣ 85
```

South opened four hearts in first seat and bought the contract unexpectedly given East's strong hand and excellent shape.

West led the king of spades and upon seeing dummy switched to a passive trump. Declarer won in hand as East pitched a low club and continued with the queen of diamonds taken by East. With diamond tricks visible in dummy and the ace of hearts as an entry, it was clear for the defence to cash out. East therefore switched to the ace of clubs. The other three players followed with the eight, seven and two of clubs, East-West playing upside-down signals.

East now had to decide whether the fourth defensive trick was in clubs or spades. East-West play low encourage, but declarer's accurate falsecard of the eight of clubs misled East. Consequently, when she eventually played a spade declarer could ruff and claim ten tricks by crossing to the ace of hearts and discarding her losing club on the top diamonds.

Several decisions went wrong for East-West here. In the pass-out seat, East could have taken a decision to compete with a take-out double or four no-trumps—an action which several pairs found. Perhaps with three aces she thought four hearts would be defeated and five of anything might be a worse contract than defending. A takeout double would have landed East-West in their making five diamonds–perhaps doubled.

On defence, a spade continuation by West at trick two would have clarified the situation for East-West, while a trump switch did not serve much purpose. Finally, after East won the ace of diamonds and switched to the ace of clubs, declarer had done well to conceal the five of clubs, but East should not have been taken in. With ♣J75, West would violently discourage with the jack, so the seven was either West's lowest (making a club continuation the correct play as declarer would be marked with the five) or her highest from ♣75, giving declarer ♣KJ8 and almost certainly a singleton spade and ten sure tricks (and a 1♥ opener rather than a 4♥ opener besides). Whatever the rationale, the decision cost East-West the match (and a place on the team), as most East-West pairs either found the making five diamonds or defeated four hearts doubled.

How much of an effect did tiredness and/or tension have on the decisions on this board? Was there insufficient 'match-training' by the pair prior to this event? Any number of factors could have contributed to the result on this board, but it seems likely to me that had the board occurred earlier in the event at a point with less fatigue and less pressure, a different outcome would have been likely.

How to get match fit

Athletes address the phenomena of 'match fitness' by participating in overload training and by playing in some lesser competitions before the main competition of the year. What this meant for me in shooting was that if my match was sixty shots long, I used to regularly practice shooting matches at least twice as long. With everything else going on in competition, the last thing you need is fatigue contributing to a sub-optimal performance. I once heard an Olympic champion shooter say, "your competition day should be the easiest match of the year".

How does this apply to bridge tournaments which are multi-match and multi-day events? If we consider that most national events are made up of several multi-board matches per day, then our practice and preparation for these events needs to prepare us to be able to play at our best right up until the last card of the day. In the same way that I regularly fired more shots in training than the length of my match required, in preparing for these types of events playing multiple 30+ board matches in practice sessions will help ensure you are prepared for the rigours of competition.

Overload training on its own is insufficient, and I have also discussed in previous chapters the concept of taking a mental break when a bad board occurs or when one of the partnership has a failure at the table that may cause a loss of concentration on future boards. The same tactics may also be used to provide a mental break in the latter part of the match to make sure you are re-focussed for the last few boards. A toilet break or a water run at board ten of a fourteen or sixteen board match might not be physically necessary for a player, but this break can provide the time for a little mental rest allowing you to avoid lapses in the vital last few boards.

Nutrition and hydration

A second consideration when ensuring you are match fit is nutrition. Think about what you are eating during the day when playing a bridge competition so as to ensure your energy levels are maintained for the whole day.

Breakfast

In my opinion the importance of breakfast should not be underestimated. Many investigations have shown that concentration can be affected when doing intellectual activities in the morning without having had breakfast previously. A proper breakfast helps to keep mental performance at an optimal level in that moment of the day according to tests on memory and attention.[1]

Lunch

A heavy meal at lunch will pull the blood from your brain to your stomach to help with digestion making you feel slightly drowsy. This can detract from your concentration. This lack of alertness could cause some mistakes that wouldn't have happened had you been fully awake. A light lunch is better – something sufficient to keep your blood sugar levels high but not so much that the meal has a negative effect on your concentration.

During the day

Maintaining hydration is also critical for success and waiting until you are thirsty means you are already dehydrated. Keeping a steady supply of fluids is an important aid for keeping concentration levels and alertness.

In long matches where energy levels might flag towards the end of the day, some players like to have sugary drinks or sweets to give a burst of energy. While it's true that sugary hits during the day will give short term energy, this dose of energy is almost always followed by a drop. It is far better to consume food at mealtimes that provides a slow release of energy throughout the day. However, energy boosts can be obtained from cereal bars, fruits, raisins or other dried fruits, nuts (almonds, e.g.), and chocolate. In all cases, moderate quantities should be taken.

---

1   Chess and Nutrition: How to feed a Chess Grandmaster. Robert Baglione 2007

The advantages of being match fit

Match fitness is all about improving your prospects of winning—translating training form into competition success. It's why top tennis players often lose in the early rounds of a grand slam when they haven't played enough matches leading into the tournament. Their practice form is good, they know how to hit the ball, but when the chips are down, they sometimes lose simply because their opponent (who may not be as highly ranked) is just more 'match fit'. When you play well in practice leading into an event but falter in the main match because your preparation hasn't set you up properly for competition, it might be because you aren't match fit.

Knowing that your preparation has made you match fit going into a competition can give you an enormous confidence boost, and the benefit of this in a close match can be the difference between victory and defeat. Making the right decision on this board at the end of a long day when North bid four-spades doubled over South's pre-empt gave our side (as the defense) a 10-imp swing:

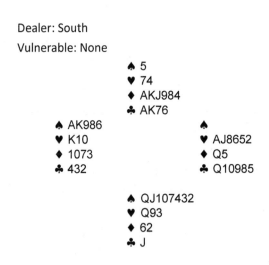

Dealer: South
Vulnerable: None

```
                    ♠ 5
                    ♥ 74
                    ♦ AKJ984
                    ♣ AK76
      ♠ AK986                    ♠
      ♥ K10                      ♥ AJ8652
      ♦ 1073                     ♦ Q5
      ♣ 432                      ♣ Q10985
                    ♠ QJ107432
                    ♥ Q93
                    ♦ 62
                    ♣ J
```

West has little option other than to pass over three spades since double would be take-out. North with a powerhouse in the minors but no fit for partner's spades elected to bid four spades, which is a fair action since partner may be able to throw some losers on the minor suit cards. Sitting East I had an interesting decision—is four spades a pre-emptive 'save' or a legitimate bid intended to make or a bit from both columns? Four no-trumps for takeout would have been an option in our system showing the two-suited hand I held. Partner clearly might have been stuck for a take-out double with a flat hand with three low spades. However, I elected to pass smoothly and partner happily doubled, which is now penalty.

West made the risky but spectacularly successful lead of the king of hearts followed by a low heart to my ace. I returned the two of hearts for partner to ruff who then exited a club won by dummy's ace. With ♠AK98 left, partner had to win three more trump tricks for plus 500 to our side against minus 50 at the other table where the defence made a different lead.

Having the courage to make the right bid or play at the end of an event when you might be either tired or under pressure shows you have the right mindset. Often it is easy to try and avoid error rather than create winning positions. It would have been all too easy for West to think "well four spades is going down, no need to try anything too risky" and lead a boring minor suit here, despite the king of hearts lead potentially being the winning choice. Being in the right frame of mind makes finding the risky (but successful) bid or play much easier at the table. On this deal, West's lead of the heart king was the only lead to enable the defence to defeat the contract so comprehensively. A 'safe' minor suit lead would have allowed declarer to pitch hearts on the minor suit winners for eight tricks—still a good score for the defence, but it is all those extra IMPs that can create the difference between a good score and a great score.

Being able to concentrate properly and find the right play at the end of a long match is an important factor for success in long tournaments. Many players are not playing at their usual standard at the end of a match or event, where tiredness can cause even the best players to make simple errors. Being the player or pair who 'plays tough' at the business end will make a big difference to your long-term success in the game.

Chapter 11

Summary

"Be humble, hungry and always be the hardest worker in the room."

– Dwayne Johnson, professional wrestler and actor

This book has discussed a wide range of techniques which are available to assist players with the mental side of the game. Using some or all of these tools can help you with improving your performance at the bridge table and get more out of the game that you love.

At the outset I began by discussing the usefulness of mental management tools as well as the impact nerves can have on performance and explained the basic principles behind why this happens. I suggested some tactics that players can employ to mitigate or prevent nerves causing a negative impact on performance. The first of these was warming up before the game to ensure simple errors are not made on the first few boards of the day. I also outlined how basic preparation and having a routine can assist with ensuring a good performance. I went on to describe the factors that can cause a player to feel under pressure in a match and how using segment goals can assist with focussing the mind on specific tasks to reduce the feeling of pressure.

The importance of bringing a positive attitude to the bridge table and how critical it is for your 'self-talk' to be constructive were both highlighted as key elements for success. While I accept that using positive affirmations is not for everyone, I explained how I found them useful and how they work. Furthermore, I stressed the advantages which can be gained from talking about your good performances to reinforce a positive mindset rather than focussing discussion on mistakes. Since negative self-talk can be extremely detrimental to your performance, I described a methodology for stopping negative thinking for those players who need additional help in this area.

A key mental tool used extremely widely is mental rehearsal. Mental rehearsal is most effective when performed in a relaxed state and I described how mental rehearsal and relaxation exercises could assist with addressing a variety of factors including nerves, negativity, learning techniques and so on.

As shown by a survey of top Australian bridge players, concentration is a key factor in success or failure at the bridge table. In Chapter 4, I talked about 'focus' at the table. I outlined the many kinds of distractions which can happen at a bridge event—both internal and external—and how to prepare for and address these to ensure you don't make a mistake if and when they occur. I also described some methods you may wish to employ to deal with distractions and the need to get your partner on board with your methods. Finally, I described the use of 'cue words' to get your mind back on track quickly after an event which might distract you has occurred.

The chapter on comfort zones illustrated how players might make errors when taken outside their usual environment or when they are performing above or below their normal expectations. It considered strategies to deal with these circumstances and to help change your comfort zone. It also stressed the importance of strong technical skills to reduce the likelihood of errors when under pressure.

For those players who are keen to improve their performance in the long term, I have taken commonly used approaches in sport and outlined how to use these in bridge to set goals and evaluate your performance. I stressed the significance of using a data-based approach to performance analysis, particularly when deciding whether or not to make technical changes to a partnership's system agreements.

Finally, I looked at the concept of 'match fitness' and the consequences which might arise when a player who is not 'match fit' reaches the final stages of an event. I suggested players could undertake an intensive training period to assist with preparation for a long arduous tournament and I highlighted the importance that nutrition and hydration play in assisting with performance during a tournament. Let me finish with a final high-pressure hand from a recent tournament:

Dealer: South

Vulnerable: None

North
- ♠ 32
- ♥ AKJ
- ♦ QJ6
- ♣ AK1073

South
- ♠ AJ54
- ♥ Q98764
- ♦ K
- ♣ 85

West	North	East	South
			1♥
Pass	2♣[1]	Pass	2♥[2]
Pass	3♥[3]	Pass	4♥[4]
Pass	4NT[5]	Pass	5♣[6]
Pass	5♦[7]	Pass	6♦[8]
Pass	6♥	All Pass	

1 - Two-over-one game force

2 - Six or more hearts

3 - Slam try

4 - Minimum hand

5 - Keycard

6 - One or four keycards

7 - Queen of trumps ask

8 - Queen of trumps and king of diamonds

Playing two-over-one, South elected to open this hand one heart, rather than a weak two since they held a four-card spade suit. Despite the lack of co-operation from South after the slam-try of three hearts, North considered their hand worth one more attempt and pressed on with keycard, propelling their side to the fair slam.

When West led the king of spades, how should South approach the play?

Clearly declarer will be quickly defeated if they try to knock out the ace of diamonds, so the clubs must be set up to provide some tricks. Likewise, trumps will need to break evenly as declarer will need to ruff a spade in the dummy later in the hand.

Our declarer played too quickly, drawing two rounds of trumps and then realised that the contract could no longer be made. Even after hearts broke 2-2 and clubs broke 3-3 (being established with one ruff), the only direct way back to dummy was by expending dummy's last trump, and two club discards were not enough. Declarer had to lose two tricks in the endgame to go one down.

Since declarer needed to cross to dummy with the second round of hearts (leaving a third heart in dummy to ruff a losing spade), slowing down and planning ahead would have allowed declarer to arrive at the conclusion that playing on clubs early was required. The best line is to win the lead, play ace, king and a third club, ruffing with the heart nine. If clubs break 3-3, all you need now is trumps 2-2, allowing you to throw a diamond and spade on the clubs and ruff a spade at the end.

If clubs are 4-2 (and you don't suffer an overruff), you still have chances: cross back to dummy with a trump (the first round that has been played), ruff a fourth club with the heart eight, back to dummy with a second round of trumps (assume they break) and throw the king of diamonds on the fifth club. The stage is now set for a ruffing finesse through East's ace of diamonds to set up one discard for a losing spade (and to ruff the final spade in dummy as before). The full deal was as follows, meaning that any line involving establishing the clubs early would have worked:

```
              ♠ 32
              ♥ AKJ
              ♦ QJ6
              ♣ AK1073
♠ KQ86                      ♠ 1097
♥ 32                        ♥ 105
♦ 10653                     ♦ A9742
♣ J92                       ♣ Q64
              ♠ AJ54
              ♥ Q98764
              ♦ K
              ♣ 85
```

This was a hand that was well within South's ability to make with clear thinking at trick one. Instead, South took a line that could never work without some extremely lucky distribution of the cards. Perhaps the pressure of being in a difficult contract caused him to fail? Maybe a mistake on a previous hand was on his mind and he didn't focus properly here. Maybe he was distracted by thoughts about his decision to open the hand rather than passing. Whatever the reason, failing to capitalise when presented with this type of hand is the difference between reaching your goals and being back with the pack. Using the mental management tools in this book would have given South a better chance of foreseeing the problem and achieving the satisfaction of bringing home a tricky slam.

I hope that the range of mental tools described in this book will help you to think more clearly and choose the right path to make hands like the one above so that you can achieve more success and enjoyment at the bridge table.

Appendix 1

Autogenic Training Program

There are several useful websites that describe autogenic training scripts. I am including some information here on the script I used, but I encourage you to do your own research.

I prefer to do this exercise at night before sleep, but you can do this at any time you choose. When doing the program at night you may fall asleep before you complete the entire exercise. This is perfectly ok. You will gradually progress and be able to achieve the relaxed state more rapidly over time. If you are concerned that you are not getting through the visualisation or rehearsal sessions that you are aiming for, you can always run these with a basic relaxation program (see Appendix 2) at another time in the day.

The anomaly in the text you will see is the line "my forehead is cool". I think this comes from the idea that people keep a cool head under pressure. Whatever the reason, all the texts use this line but none of them seem to talk about repeating it multiple times.

The exercise takes about 15 - 20 minutes to complete. You will be able to achieve a level of relaxation more quickly as you become more familiar with the exercise and your body becomes accustomed to the relaxation process. If you are struggling to get the feeling of heaviness in the limbs, you may find that applying some tension to the muscle before relaxing it will assist.

It is very useful to record this exercise (or get someone to put the instructions on tape), especially if you are planning on doing the session during the daytime so that you can reawaken and reenergise the body at the end.

Process - First 2 - 4 weeks

Lie comfortably on a mat or a mattress.

Close your eyes and start with a few deep abdominal breaths - stomach breathing (breathe in through nose and out through a relaxed mouth).

As you breathe, focus on your breathing and feel your body becoming more relaxed. Try to focus on your breathing and empty your mind of other thoughts.

Direct your attention to your right arm. Think about how your right arm is feeling heavy and warm. Repeat this to yourself 3 - 4 times. Feel how your right arm is sinking into the mat and feels heavy.

Continue to breathe deeply as you now focus on your left arm. Feel how your left arm feels heavy and warm. Repeat to yourself "my left arm is heavy and warm". Do this 3 - 4 times. Feel how your left arm is sinking into the mat and feels heavy.

Now focus on your right leg. Feel how your right leg feels heavy and warm. Repeat to yourself "my right leg is heavy and warm". Do this 3 - 4 times. Feel how your right leg is sinking into the mat and feels heavy.

Continue to breathe deeply as you now focus on your left leg. Feel how your left leg feels heavy and warm. Repeat to yourself "my left leg is heavy and warm". Do this 3 - 4 times. Feel how your left leg is sinking into the mat and feels heavy.

Focus on your hips. Feel how your hips feel heavy and warm. Repeat to yourself "my hips are heavy and warm" 3 - 4 times. Feel your hips sinking into the mat and feel the heaviness.

Now focus on your torso and stomach. Feel how your stomach feels heavy and warm as you continue to breathe slowly and rhythmically. Repeat to yourself "my stomach is heavy and warm" 3 - 4 times.

Say "My forehead is cool".

Focus on your neck and shoulders. Feel how your neck and shoulders are heavy and warm and your body is totally relaxed.

Say "at any time I choose, I can return to this relaxed state by taking 1 - 2 deep abdominal breaths".

Continue to breathe and enjoy the feeling of relaxation in your body. If you are doing this at night you can continue to breathe and you will just drift off to sleep. If you are doing this during the day, you will need to re-awaken the body.

(if you are taping this, wait for 2 - 3 minutes before continuing)

Re-awakening the body

Soon I am going to count from 1 - 5 to re-awaken the body and as I count you will feel more and more energised and your body will become more and more alert.

One - with each inhalation you are feeling more and more awake, and fresher and alert.

Two - continue to breathe a bit more quickly as you feel more and more energy.

Three - inhale and exhale - you are feeling the energy coming back to your body.

Four - you are ready to open your eyes, feeling renewed and ready to complete any task.

Five - you feel completely refreshed and energised, yet relaxed and comfortable.

Open your eyes now.

Process beyond 2 - 4 weeks

You need to judge how you are progressing before starting this next phase. If you are finding you are able to relax and clear the mind using the first stage as described above, then you are ready to move to the next phase.

In this phase we are going to work on the concentration and focus skills. In this section, you will focus on a non-emotive object or place of your choosing. This object will be a cue that you can use visually to help you re-focus and concentrate the mind when you are competing. Picturing it when competing will also help you to relax.

So to begin....

Work through the stage 1 process for relaxation.

Now start to visualise your object or place. Picture it as a whole. Now work through the object or place in detail from the top to the bottom and from the side to the side. Visualise as much detail as you can. Picture how the object or place feels, the texture of it. Remember to continue to breathe normally during this.

Now let the image go and continue to breathe as you focus on the visualisation goal you have for today. Picture yourself performing in the bridge scenario with the desired outcome. It is helpful to repeat the visualisation multiple times to imprint this on the mind, either in this session or in future sessions.

Appendix 2

Basic Relaxation Program[1]

The following script can be put on to a tape if preferred.

"Settle yourself into a comfortable, seated position. Adjust your posture so that the chair is completely supporting your weight. Close your eyes and begin by taking three long, slow breaths, focusing on the feeling of relaxation each time as you breathe out. Notice with each breath that you take that there is a moment of relief with the exhalation of each breath.

"Continue to breathe slowly, enjoying the feeling of relaxation and as you do try to associate that pleasant feeling with an increasing heaviness in each muscle group within your body.

"Let that feeling begin in the muscles around your forehead and face and then let it spread very slowly down through your neck and shoulders. Continue the spread of relaxation taking at least two minutes to spread it down through your whole body.

"When you have relaxed each and every muscle group within your body, take two more deep breaths and then enjoy the feeling of relaxation.

"When you wish to 're-awaken' count slowly backwards from 5 to 1 stretching your muscles as you do so. You will then feel refreshed and rested."

---

1   Adapted from material presented to the Australian Shooting Team by the sports psychologist Graham Winter

Appendix 3

The Annual Training Plan

Taking performance goals and putting them into an overall plan for improvement is something for the serious player to consider. Those who aspire to represent their country may wish to follow the example of elite athletes who usually have a well-defined annual training plan. The annual plan for my shooting year sets out the competition periods, peak training periods, rest periods, fitness training periods, experimenting periods and other key events during the year. It also included annual goals, and goals specifically for individual competitions and training. As outlined in chapter eight, goals should be both score-based and technique or performance-based.

It is easy to say you want to win everything you enter, but that is not always practical. For example, swimmers usually have periods of highly intensive training after which they taper for competitions that are important to them. It would generally be unrealistic to expect a swimmer who was in intensive training to win against a swimmer who has tapered for competition if both are of roughly equal ability. The swimmer who has tapered is in 'peak' condition for their event.

Similarly, in bridge at times we may wish to make changes to our system or methods or we may be trying out a new partnership.

As an example, in my home country Australia, the annual bridge calendar is quite busy with competitions. At the time of writing there are many national events during the year beginning with a major national event called the Summer Festival in January and concluding with the playoffs for the national teams in late November/early December. Most countries have equally busy bridge calendars.

For an international level player developing their annual training and competition program, consideration must be given to the timing of national events, which may be used as lead-in preparation for international events. Inclusion of some other local events may also be considered as useful preparation for competition or required to earn a living for the players who play professionally with sponsors. There is also that minor factor of actually making sure you win the selection trials—not much point having a goal to win the World Championships if you don't make the team, is there? Factoring changes to system or methods or even to partnerships into this calendar can influence performance in the short term and it is important to keep sight of the long-term goal.

For state level players who participate in club and/or state events, there are key events such as club championships, local competitions and some national events. Each player is different and each will have events they consider to be the most important for them. It might just be beating the pair with whom you have a friendly rivalry in the weekly club duplicate.

The level you aspire to will determine the degree of detail required in your annual plan.

The following is a rough guide to help you get started. Get a one-year calendar (either electronic or paper) and mark up the following on it.

1. Identify the key competitions that are most important to you in the year(s) ahead. Try and pick two or three events you really want to do well at.

2. Identify the periods in the year when you will have breaks (holidays, family commitments, work commitments, Christmas, etc.).

3. Identify the periods that you may wish to use to experiment with new conventions or system changes or to play with a different partner. Note that experimenting should occur well in advance of key competitions to allow time to ensure the changes are going to be effective.

4. For the key competitions, mark out any lead-up events you wish to use to gain competition practice. Identify dates/times that you and your partner will set aside to do bidding/play practice. BBO is a superb resource to use for both partnership bidding and practice matches.

At the end of every year, reviewing how well your training plan worked allows you to measure how successful you were when compared to the goals you set yourself. You can also identify any changes you might wish to make in your training and preparation for the following year. For example, you might find you need more time to practice system changes before the major events for your year.

Planning your year keeps you focussed on what is important too. If your goal is to win the World Championships, you need to develop a multi-year plan with the key competitions for the next four years identified.

Appendix 4 - Sample Spreadsheet Analysis

Analysis of performance on hands played using hand records can enable errors to be tabulated into a number of broad categories to determine the main areas of weakness for the player.

Keep notes on the hand records as you classify the errors to enable further analysis later.

Date	Boards	B	J	DP	Def	L	C	S
3-Jul	27	1	1	3	0	2	0	0
5-Jul	27	3	0	2	2	1	1	0
6-Jul	56	2	2	5	3	1	0	2
7-Jul	54	1	2	6	3	2	0	2
10-Jul	27	1	2	2	1	1	0	0
17-Jul	27	0	3	3	2	0	0	1
23-Jul	56	3	2	5	2	1	0	0
24-Jul	54	5	2	6	3	0	1	2
27-Jul	27	1	1	2	1	0	0	1
30-Jul	56	3	2	4	2	1	0	3
31-Jul	54	2	2	6	3	2	0	1
Totals	465	22	19	44	22	11	2	12

Legend: B-Bidding; J-Judgement; DP-Declarer Play; Def-Defence; L-Lead; C-Concentration; S-System

From the above table it is clear that 'Declarer Play' is the area causing this player the most concern. Having identified the broad area for attention, further analysis should be undertaken to determine if there are particular contracts or hand types which are the area of weakness. For example, contracts can initially be broken into two broad types—no-trump and suit contracts.

Review the hand records for the above data and put the hands into these two categories. Let's say out of the 44 hands you find 26 of them were no-trump contracts and 18 were suit contracts. You have a place to start working to improve your game, since you now know that playing in no-trumps is an area of weakness for you.

You could start work on improving this area by reading some books on how to play no-trump contracts or do some practice using one of the computer programs available or you could get some coaching from a bridge teacher.

You might also examine whether you should have been playing in a suit rather than in no-trumps. You might also look at whether your system is preventing you from finding your best contract. For example, you may find that including a forcing no-trump methodology in your system agreements allows you to play in two of a minor making rather than one no-trump going off.

The above is a simple way to start using data analysis to improve your game by allowing you to identify where your bridge requires improvement.

There is a wide scope for adding complexity and detail to the above generalised scheme, but as with most things, it's important to start with something simple and expand on it as necessary rather than trying to do something complex from the outset.

Glossary

IMPs - International Match Points, used in teams matches

VPs - Victory Points

BBO - Bridge Base Online — www.bridgebase.com. An online program for smartphones, tablets and computers for playing with a partner, against robots or for general practice.

uBid - uBid is an app on bidding developed by NewInBridge and is meant for smartphones and tablets. uBid allows users to practice and improve their bidding skills.

Acknowledgements

When I originally thought about writing a book, I had no idea how long it would take. Like any endeavour of this type, there have been many who have offered me support and encouragement to continue.

Thanks go first of all to my husband, John, for his great support throughout my competitive pursuits in shooting, and now bridge. My achievements would not have been possible without you.

To my brilliant proof-reader Liam Milne, who offered so many fabulous suggestions and comments, checked out all the hands and made many other improvements, I thank you from the bottom of my heart. Your enthusiasm for the project was an inspiration to me. Thank you to Ron Klinger for kindly agreeing to write a foreword, and for proof-reading my final draft. Your input was truly appreciated.

Thank you to my brother Simon and his wife Heather for their help with proof-reading and photography.

Thank you to Sally, Ray and Martin at Masterpoint Press for your patience and assistance on the road to publication.

Many thanks also to David Morgan who first provided the germ of an idea to start applying my knowledge of mental tools to the bridge world. Thanks also for his excellent tips on partnership principles.

Thank you to Bill Jacobs for providing me with his data analysis on his partnership methods when he switched to Fantunes.

A big thank you to everyone who has read my articles in the various magazines in which they have been published and provided me with such nice feedback.

Finally, thanks to all the unnamed players who feature in the hands in the book. I couldn't have come up with such interesting hands to illustrate the various themes without such great opponents to play against. I look forward to our next contest at the bridge table.

Kim Frazer, Melbourne 2019

About the author

Kim Frazer represented Australia on numerous occasions in target shooting winning three Commonwealth Games gold medals, numerous Australian titles and other awards. Since retiring from international shooting competition in 2006, Kim continued her involvement with the sport as both a coach and administrator.

Although Kim had played an occasional hand of 'kitchen bridge' while at university in the 1970s, it wasn't until 2005 that she returned to competitive bridge with a newfound focus. She first represented Australia in 2018 as a member of the Australian Women's Team at the Commonwealth Nations Bridge Tournament in Surfers Paradise and the World Bridge Federation Championships in Orlando, Florida.

She has written a series of articles on mental tools for bridge for the Australian Bridge Federation newsletter, and more recently Australian Bridge. These articles are being translated for publication in France's Le Bridgeur.

Kim has also created a website where new articles will appear. Visit the website at www.havingthementaledge.com

CPSIA information can be obtained
at www.ICGtesting.com
Printed in the USA
LVHW050934140120
643554LV00003B/474